APARTMENTS

ALSO BY MARIETTE HIMES GOMEZ

Houses

Rooms

APART

MENTS

DEFINING STYLE

MARIETTE HIMES GOMEZ

WITH
CHRISTINE PITTEL

PHOTOGRAPHS BY
SCOTT FRANCES

HarperCollins books may be purchased for educational, business, or sales promotional use. For information, please write: Special Markets Department, HarperCollins Publishers, 10 East 53rd Street, New York, NY 10022.

FIRST EDITION

Designed by Joel Avirom, Jason Snyder, and Meghan Day Healey

Library of Congress Cataloging-in-Publication Data

Gomez, Mariette Himes.
  Apartments: defining style/Mariette Himes Gomez with Christine Pittel;
  photographs by Scott Frances.—1st ed.
     p. cm.
  ISBN 978-0-06-167236-1
  1. Apartments. 2. Interior decoration. I. Pittel, Christine. II. Frances, Scott, 1958–
III. Title.
NK2195.A6G66 2009
747'.88314—dc22

                                                          2008045709

         09 10 11 12 13   ❖/RRD   10 9 8 7 6 5 4 3 2 1

I dedicate this book to all my wonderful clients;

you know who you are.

CONTENTS

Growing up in a house in Michigan, the idea of living in an apartment seemed impossibly glamorous. The images in my head came straight out of the movies. Even now, I can think of several enticing examples of New York real estate that could convince me to pack my bags and move right in: Dick Powell and Myrna Loy's art deco charmer in *The Thin Man*, Katharine Hepburn and Spencer Tracy's Turtle Bay duplex in *Adam's Rib*, Mia Farrow's rambling wood-paneled Central Park West apartment in *Hannah and Her Sisters*, even Audrey Hepburn's barely furnished third-floor walk-up in a townhouse on the Upper East Side. Well, maybe not the walk-up.

But as someone who has lived both in houses and apartments, I can say there are some advantages to apartment living. In buildings of a certain caliber, packages appear magically at your door. Visitors are announced. A kindly doorman procures taxis and even has an umbrella handy to hold over you in the rain. Unfortunate mishaps involving boilers and leaky pipes are handled by others. There is a staff on hand to see to your needs. My building manager actually helped me trim my Christmas tree when I ran out of time before a party.

Most apartments are found in densely populated urban environments. The apartments shown in this book are mainly in New York, with two forays down to Florida and a jaunt across the Atlantic to London. Some are in mature buildings with elaborate architectural detail. Others are part of newer construction where the architect took a more streamlined approach. Before you begin to decorate, you must read the character of your doors, walls, and windows. Notice where

INTRODUCTION

the natural light is coming from. Strong sunlight on a cloudy day can change the colors in an apartment's interior. I like to take advantage of this by not doing exaggerated window treatments, as well as providing for ample lamplight to compensate for the cloudy or rainy days.

Apartments often have more enclosed space than houses, and there are tricks that can make them feel a little more expansive. If you can create a connecting thread—such as doors that align so your eye goes to the farthest point—you can make a space seem larger. A narrow hallway that leads into a larger bedroom will make that bedroom feel so much loftier. Yet the most important trick has nothing to do with doors and walls and does not require a contractor. It involves only you. You must learn how to edit your possessions. Any room, small or large, will appear smaller if it is cluttered. Keep it simple, and your apartment will feel like a bigger box.

The first thing to do, even before you begin decorating, is to decide how you want to use a room. Will this be a private retreat or a space that should accommodate large groups of people? That will help determine the design. I love mixing styles of the past with those of the present. I think rooms, particularly in an apartment, are more interesting and inviting if this is done well. Don't be afraid to hang a contemporary painting over a Chippendale chair.

When purchasing furniture, strive for lasting quality—unless your personality requires constant change. If this is the case, I would still advise you to invest in serious staples and then feel free to play with the accessories around them. Changing a wall color or a window curtain is often easier than replacing a dining table or a sofa. These large objects are difficult to get in and out of an apartment and often involve special delivery charges. If you do decide to replace furnishings, give them a second life in that extra room, the kitchen, or the bath.

Consider how color and texture on walls, trim, ceilings, floors, and upholstery will contribute to the mood. I like to mix various tones of the same pale colors to create calm. Strong, bold colors can be very effective, but be aware that they can also make a room feel smaller.

Adequate lighting is essential if you want all your best efforts to show. Never underestimate the value of a table or floor lamp. I'm a firm believer in dimmer switches, one of the quickest ways to create atmosphere in even the smallest space.

Tabletops are another opportunity to add interest and build character. Display objects that matter to you. The idea is to create a multilayered space that is steeped in personality. Details matter. Decorating actually starts at the front door, with the doorknob. Pay attention to everything your hand will touch.

If you need motivation before starting your own project, you might try a little research. Take a class in furniture styles, or thumb through books on color. Anyone can learn how to draw a rudimentary floor plan. If all this sounds too complicated, simply get out a DVD. Study the sets in early black-and-white movies or extravagant films like *Marie Antoinette* or *The Madness of King George*. Somehow they always strike an intriguing note of color, drama, and mood.

Still searching for inspiration? Just turn the page.

1 | DARK AND LIGHT

If, like these clients, you're lucky enough to own an apartment in one of the great New York apartment houses designed by Rosario Candela in the 1920s, half my job is already done. I won't have to rework the architecture because it will already be superb. The windows will stretch to the floor, with French doors opening onto a balcony that makes you feel as if you're in Paris. The ceilings will be elegantly high, and the proportions of the rooms will be gracious.

Yet this apartment had something even more unusual. The living room walls had been painted in the most extraordinary faux finish to mimic burled wood. Look at the grain! You'd think it was real. But the wife was worried. She was afraid the room was too dark, but her husband didn't want to change it. He was relying on me to make it right. As we went back and forth about whether the faux paneling should stay or go, my mind was racing. I said, "Let's make the whole apartment all about dark and light. The walls are dark, but everything else will be light."

Now the entrance hall is a serene white, which sets the stage for that magnificent trompe l'oeil paneling. In an apartment, the first real opportunity for impact is just inside the front door, and I always try to make the most of it. What emotion do you want people to feel? I wanted a guest to feel tranquil and calm, and then be struck by the drama of that dazzling faux paneling. The entrance hall is very

PREVIOUS SPREAD
There's nothing complicated about this arrangement of furniture—two matching sofas and a cane-back chair. While I didn't want to take your attention away from the beautiful walls, I couldn't resist one amusing detail—the luxurious bullion fringe, which makes the sofas feel very French.

OPPOSITE
The entrance hall is deliberately simple. The walls, moldings, and ceiling are painted the same white, just in slightly different finishes, to create a sense of quiet as you enter. Then your eye is immediately drawn from the light hall to the darker living room, which is framed by the doorway.

plain, so as not to compete. The only furniture is an English mahogany bench, where you could set down a briefcase, under the curve of the staircase. All those lovely staircases in Manhattan duplex apartments feel like movie sets to me.

In the living room, the trompe l'oeil paneling is framed by a beautiful crown molding original to the building, which I painted white, along with the ceiling. I also brought in a pure white marble mantel, very classical, to suit the architecture. Something interesting happens to the paneling against all that white. Suddenly it doesn't look old-fashioned anymore but starts to become an abstraction in itself, almost as if it were a work of contemporary art. I'm so glad we didn't paint it out. All it needed was a little restoration. My daughter, Brooke Gomez, who worked with me on this project, tracked down the man who originally painted it in Paris, and we flew him in to do a little touch-up.

The faux finish takes center stage and the furniture recedes, but it doesn't disappear. The beauty of this room lies in the relationship of paneling and objects and furniture. There's light and dark wherever you look. I covered the sofas in white so they would balance the fireplace and play off the dark floor. The sofas are twins, which sets up a basic symmetry. I get really fussy if things don't feel balanced. Every piece has to find its proper place. A 1940s French mirror hangs on one side of the fireplace. Most people would say that if you have a mirror

ABOVE
When I spotted this 1940s French coffee table at an antiques show, I bought it immediately. I loved the mirrored top, hand-painted with flowers. A glass vase is filled with spirea, which adds a few more trailing tendrils. There's something so fresh and delicate about those confetti-like petals.

OPPOSITE
It's hard to believe this is not three-dimensional paneling. In fact, it's paint that has been faux-finished to resemble various woods. Even the intricately painted "molding" that seems to frame the 1940s French mirror is completely flat.

on one side you need one on the other to match. But I couldn't put a large mirror to the left of the fireplace because it would get in the way of a hidden door. So I balanced the mirror with a painting. That makes sense to me because I believe a mirror is not just a mirror. It gives you another view of a room, like a painting. In fact, it's really a device to reflect light and space.

When choosing a chair, my eye always goes to something that has strong lines, like the English Regency chair that faces the fireplace. I like the idea of a cane back. It lets the air through. It breathes. In the upholstered pieces, I needed a little softness to counteract all the strict geometrics in the faux finish. The sofas have rounded edges and soft cushions. And then the mirrored coffee table with its delicate etching looks so pretty against all this strength and seriousness. This is one of those divine rooms that just came together and formed a pleasing composition, like any good work of art.

I put a desk by the window because I think it's smart to animate a living room by making it do more than one thing. You can take a phone call and get some work done. Otherwise a living room is just a reception room, and you have no real reason to go into it unless you have guests. Especially in an apartment, it makes sense to have rooms that are multifunctional. Here, the dining room doubles as a library. Interestingly, we managed to light it without resorting to the typical

OPPOSITE

The English Regency period produced some of the most beautiful furniture. Look at that lovely lyre detail on the writing table, which I've set by the window to take advantage of the light. I didn't want to encumber the windows with elaborate curtains or create any distraction near that elegant cornice. The curtain rod is so simple it practically disappears.

RIGHT

The silent end of this living room comes alive with these magnificent pieces of furniture and the classy pale glass lamp. Well-chosen quality furniture always demands your attention.

chandelier. Instead, we put picture lights over each bookcase and two little lamps each on the bottom shelves near the dining table. All the light is coming from the perimeter and it works, combined with two reading lamps by the club chairs.

I'll tell you why I hung a mirror behind one of the chairs. There's a wonderful American quilt hanging in the hallway just opposite, and when you walk into this room, the mirror reflects the quilt and gives you another chance to look at it.

ABOVE AND OPPOSITE

A pedestal table makes so much sense for dining. With fewer legs, you can often accommodate more chairs. Of course, this dining room is not dedicated just to dining; it also functions as the library. I've placed reading lights next to two comfortable chairs, which swivel so you can watch TV. When the TV is not in use, it can vanish behind closed doors.

OVERLEAF

The dining room–library challenge: the two-sided room. How to light the table without a chandelier? Picture lights over the books and a pair of lamps at counter height do the job without a chandelier in the middle of the room.

The kitchen looks as if it has always been there, but in fact it's new. The architect, Jim Joseph, was able to take down a wall and reconfigure a maid's room to make a bigger kitchen. The old-fashioned-style mahogany cabinets are totally consistent with what you might find in an apartment of this period, and the subway tile is suitably urban. Combined with white marble countertops, it reminds me of the butler's pantry in an old house.

OPPOSITE
The classic wooden cabinets in the kitchen are offset by small-scale marble tiles in a running band pattern.

ABOVE
The original kitchen and a maid's room were combined to create a new, larger scullery-style kitchen that suits the period of the apartment yet is equipped with every modern convenience. The walnut cabinets and marble countertops continue the dark and light theme. We chose a cork floor because it's easy on the feet.

OVERLEAF
The beauty of this bedroom lies in its purity: white walls, white carpet, white upholstered furniture—and then that simple iron bed, which is pure geometry.

DARK AND LIGHT

The light and dark effects continue upstairs in the master bedroom, which is a calm, restful white. The iron four-poster bed is utterly simple—no canopy, no fuss. It's like a line drawing in space. Built-in cabinets to the right of the fireplace barely interrupt the wall and keep the shell very clean. I like to keep clutter out of sight. Any room will feel larger visually if all those little possessions are kept behind closed doors. Then the eye can focus on one or two great pieces, like

OPPOSITE
Red peonies and a collection of silver-capped bottles emphasize the purity of the white wall color and the bed's simplicity, as reflected in the mirror. I love moments in a room like this.

ABOVE
The white walls set off the wood antiques, accentuating the fine lines of an American grandfather clock and an English bowfront chest.

the grandfather clock or the beautiful English bowfront chest. One reason this room looks so peaceful is that it is not crammed with furniture. The TV is tucked into a cabinet as well. The off-white wall-to-wall carpet adds a touch of softness underfoot. I repeated the same simple style of curtains as I used downstairs. Why mask those glorious windows? In a New York apartment, you want to cultivate light. Besides, if you gussied up the curtains too much, I don't think you'd see the lovely ironwork on the balconies.

Jim Joseph and I were able to reconfigure the space for the bathrooms and create two classic baths, the kind you might see at a great old hotel like the Crillon, in Paris. Brooke went down to the marble yard and personally picked out every slab. We had to steal some square footage from a closet to get a larger bathroom for him. Her bathroom is even dreamier. I love that gorgeous piece of marble behind her tub. If you have room, I always recommend putting in one piece of furniture, like a chest of drawers or a dressing table. It adds a lot of charm and somehow makes even the most urbane room feel more personal, a bit like an old English country house.

ABOVE
It's important to carve out closet space that meets your particular needs. The main thing is to take stock of what your needs are.

OPPOSITE
Built-in closets line both sides of the dressing room. We were able to tuck in a dressing table by building out the ledge under the window. Just pull the stool closer, and you can sit down to try on jewelry or apply your makeup by natural light.

No matter where you are, you should be surrounded by things you love. The objects that have meaning for you and reflect your personality have the most resonance. You need that singular touch if you want to create a warm, individual home.

OPPOSITE

There is nothing more luxurious than large expanses of marble paneling in a bathroom. To warm up the room, simply add one piece of furniture, such as that antique chest of drawers. The mirrored panel just above doubles the natural light. (I always make sure to provide adequate light in a bathroom.) If you want to make a new room look older, find a period light fixture, such as that Regency-style frosted-glass hanging lamp.

ABOVE

The husband's bathroom features a large marble shower with its own window. When he wants privacy, the solar shade can be pulled down. Built-in cabinetry offers plenty of storage. I like how the old-fashioned fixtures and traditional details, such as the contrasting border in the marble floor, give a new room a sense of age.

RIGHT

Mirrored panels on each side of the window recess expand the view—and conceal the medicine chest at the same time. It's an old trick that works beautifully.

When you have a place in London, the logical thing to do is to make it look quint-essentially English—a look that will never go out of style. For most people, a London pied-à-terre is a fantasy. But for my clients, it became a reality when they acquired this three-story flat in a London townhouse and asked me to help decorate it.

The townhouse, on one of those elegant English crescents, was built around 1880 in the style of Regency designer Thomas Hope—very pure and very classical. There's nothing quite like a twelve-foot-high ceiling for making a space feel special, even without anything in it. As soon as I saw the entrance foyer, it was clear to me that we needed a fabulous mirror. I found exactly what I wanted at the Olympia International Art & Antiques Fair. This mirror is at least six feet tall and has an unusual horseshoe shape. Facing the staircase, it reflects the window at the top and seems to double the light in the room. It hangs in the center of the wall above a large radiator. At first we considered removing the radiator or building some sort of box around it. But then my client said she actually didn't mind seeing it, because it's exactly the kind of thing you'd find in a typical English house. Frankly, it was doing the job of heating the hall very efficiently, so we decided to leave it there. I found a Regency console table—a true console, with two legs instead of four—that was

PREVIOUS SPREAD
The large-scale contemporary photograph on the wall is not just interesting to look at. It also seems to extend the space of the room. The mirror over the fireplace is a more traditional way of creating the same effect.

OPPOSITE
The scale of the furnishings had to match the lofty proportions of this entrance hall, which is why I was particularly pleased to find that tall horseshoe-shape mirror. It's flanked by hurricane sconces from Charles Edwards. The huge hanging glass light fixture was modeled on an antique original. I like the spherical shape and the antique bronze finish. The X-backed chairs flanking the Regency console are newly made in the style of conservatory chairs, with curved saddle seats.

APARTMENTS

◆

28

the perfect size to sit right over the radiator. We bolted it to the wall, and it absorbs a little of the attention and provides a convenient place to set down your keys or display a vase of flowers. Now the mirror, the table, and the radiator form a balanced composition.

All the furnishings in this apartment had to be very pure and strong, so that they could stand up to the lofty proportions of the rooms. The clients would fly over from New York, and we'd go shopping at my favorite antiques shops for just the right pieces. Most people make the mistake of thinking that if you have a large room, you need a lot of furniture. But I took the opposite approach. We bought a few good pieces to establish character, and then I surrounded them with a lot of space. The luxury in this apartment is space itself.

These clients are serious art collectors, and they chose to hang a contemporary wall-size photograph in their period drawing room. That's a very bold gesture, and it set the tone. This would be a traditional apartment with a contemporary edge. Even a fine antique, like the eighteenth-century chest to the left of the fireplace, becomes more

In the upstairs hall, we painted the walls pale gray and picked out off-white wainscoting to give the space a waist. The hall table is the kind of piece that might have appealed to Sir John Soane, the English architect who is synonymous with a distinctive neoclassical style. Most of his furniture was either over- or underscaled or exaggerated in some way. Look how skinny the table's legs are.

about shape and line when it stands isolated, on its own. It looks clean and fresh and almost modern when surrounded by negative space. Two puzzle-back chairs float in the middle of the room, which makes it easier to study the intricate pattern of the lines on their backs. It is a very modernist sensibility to objectify each piece, and when you objectify something, it has to be worth the attention—like those chairs.

The bay window is a big draw in the room, so that's where we put the seating area. All the upholstered pieces just seemed to head in that direction. It makes sense to put your sofa and chairs near the light. I love the height of the windows and accentuated this feature by hanging floor-to-ceiling curtains made of a thick, gorgeous silk. Do you see the lamps? They're tall, like the curtains. The side tables they stand on do not match. I already had two pairs—the puzzle-back chairs and the club chairs. If I had chosen a pair of side tables, it would have looked like a furniture showroom.

There's a subtlety to the colors of the fabric on the sofa and chairs—more thick, rich silks in closely matched tones of cream and taupe—yet each silk has its own texture. One's a stripe and another's a basket weave. I saved the pattern for the carpet. You don't need to bring pattern into every group of furniture, and sometimes a room feels more unified without it. Here, I was also anticipating that the clients wanted the art to be the focus.

The paint color on the walls is the richest cream you've ever seen, like the famous Devonshire clotted cream the English eat with strawberries and scones at teatime. Master colorist Donald Kaufman did the paint colors for the house. He flew over from New York, and we all met in the space and agreed on what color we thought each room

The white marble mantel in the living room is probably original to the townhouse. I bought that white overmantel mirror, a serious eighteenth-century piece with lovely proportions, to hang above it. There's something about that tall, slim rectangle over the square fireplace that's interesting to the eye. And the pedimented top is very classical, which suits the architecture.

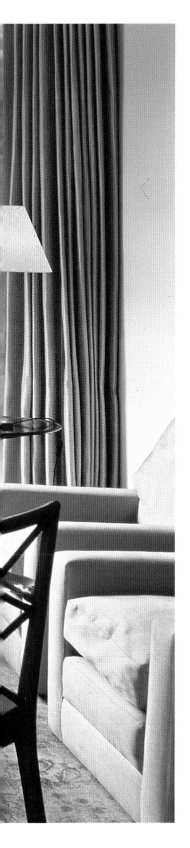

should be. Then he went off to do his alchemist thing with pigments and paint. He mixed up our custom colors and did the sample brush-outs. If one of us wasn't sure, he tried another take until everyone was satisfied. Then he painted each room with a first coat. The clients took a look, loved it, and that was that. Donald always does my paint colors. There is another reason the paint colors look so good in this apartment: The walls are made of old-fashioned plaster, not drywall. Plaster really makes a difference. It adds depth to a wall, and the more coats of paint you put on top of it, the better. It makes for softer edges.

It took us a while to figure out what color to paint the library. All we knew was that we didn't want the typical green or red. Then I suggested a deep brown-black that seems to envelop you as soon as you walk into the room. It's smoky and sophisticated and sets off the elaborate trac-ery on the plaster ceiling, which is painted chalk white. We also painted the bookcases white.

The focal point of the room is that black man-tel, in two shades of marble, which was so distinc-tive that no one wanted to replace it. I felt it was a small triumph when I found that Irish mahogany mirror, which suited it perfectly. Every piece in this

The sunlight streaming through the bay windows makes this area the perfect place to sit. I grouped the furniture around an unobtrusive glass coffee table and made sure every chair was comfortable. No particular fabric stands out. Instead the colors blend, which makes for a restful room. The silk I chose for the curtains is exceptionally thick and hangs beautifully, creating curtains resembling fluted columns.

Dark colors seem to suit the tranquil, thoughtful mood you want in a library. If the walls here were white instead of that deep, rich brown, you might not notice the delicate tracery on the ceiling. The ottoman, upholstered in creamy suede, offers a lighter note and was made to our specifications by Soane, a shop in London. The mahogany chairs are covered in traditional horsehair.

room is very individual. The sofa with the gold-painted legs is attributed to Sister Parish. The ottoman is in the style of Sir John Soane. There's a Jacques Adnet desk by the window. All these objects tell you something about the owner. Only a person of character could put all these character-filled pieces together and feel right at home.

Upstairs, the master bedroom offers another mood, very spare and simple, which brings out the bones of the room. The mantel is quite something, with those fluted pedestals to hold knickknacks (notice we left them empty). No doubt it's original to the house. I

OPPOSITE

In the master bedroom, the lovely leaded-glass window exemplifies the quirkiness of English architecture. I can just hear someone saying, "Oh, I'd like a window in that corner." It overlooks the rear garden and came equipped with that inviting window seat. We re-covered it in a bold stripe and added a cozy wing chair by the fireplace.

ABOVE

The large custom-made mahogany four-poster has such a beautiful shape that it really didn't require any further adornments. I placed a pedestal table and a pair of Danish chairs near the bay window: a lovely spot for an impromptu breakfast with the morning papers.

can't even describe the color on the walls. Is it yellow? Mustard? Ocher? Like all Donald Kaufman's colors, it changes with the light. The bed is a king-size four-poster, which of course we had made since the old ones were never that big. You'll see a wing chair by the fireplace. I deploy wing chairs with great discernment because I find the shape so powerful. They're almost statuary to me. If you want to make a moment, just bring in a wing chair. Of course, there are wing chairs and then there are exceptional wing chairs, and this one is at the top of the heap. See how the back bows out at the side? It's a very good copy of an eighteenth-century original, made by Christopher Howe, a very good English antiques dealer and furniture designer. He has a small studio where he crafts each piece by hand, to order. The sofa and the club chairs in the drawing room are also his.

The Regency table in the ground-floor dining room can accommodate two for breakfast or eight for dinner. It's a very cozy room, with that massive fireplace. On the other hand, there's nothing heavy about the chandelier. Instead of the usual ornament dripping with crystals, it's light and sleek and made of nickel. I love the octagonal shape and the pivoting

There comes a time when windows speak for themselves. Here, to enjoy the light and air, we added only roller shades for privacy. An oval English breakfront table serves as an ample desk.

candlesticks. I found it at Charles Edwards, who does some of the best lighting in London.

The kitchen was already there and we just made it better. Donald came up with that funky green for the island. We kept the hand-painted tiles around the stove and fireplace and above the banquette. Sunday lunch in England is traditionally held in the kitchen, and the

ABOVE

The table setting includes a pair of candlesticks made of rich brown 1930s Bakelite, and the china, crystal, and silver patterns were chosen for their modern simplicity as well.

OPPOSITE

I found the English Regency dining table and chairs and then thought twice about adding more mahogany with that nineteenth-century Irish mirror over the fireplace, but it all seems to work. The dark woods make the room feel even richer.

banquette provides the perfect setting. We just reupholstered it in a happier color—a celery green to complement the outside garden. The table is English oak. It's a hard choice between this and the zinc table out in the garden. To have outdoor space along with any apartment is a real treat, and I furnished the garden with a table and chairs and a chaise longue, for reading under the trees.

ABOVE

The tiles over the banquette are decorated with flowering cachepots and urns, which seem to bring the garden inside. Most people would probably have left the banquette on its own, but I think it looks even more inviting with those X-backed chairs in front, as if more guests are about to arrive.

OPPOSITE

The tiles over the cast-iron fireplace were already there, and we saw no reason to remove them. They're charming.

OVERLEAF

The worktable, painted an unusual shade of green and topped with sturdy butcher block, is a centerpiece of English kitchen design.

ABOVE

The sound of splashing water can be very soothing in
a garden. This fountain, inlaid with shells and stones,
looks like a miniature grotto.

RIGHT

What a pleasant place to read—in a chaise longue
under a tree! Hard to believe you're right in the middle
of London.

Occasionally, apartment dwellers get to expand vertically. When this family acquired the apartment above them as well as its roof, they called me—and architect Oscar Shamamian—and gave us the job of turning these three separate entities into one seamless whole. If you have a large-scale project like this, I always recommend hiring an architect to help work out the floor plan and solve any structural problems. The place was like a puzzle that we had to take apart and put back together again, reconfiguring rooms to suit new uses and creating a logical flow. Most people think it's the architect who bakes the cake, and then the designer comes in and slathers on some frosting. That's not the way I like to work. If both parties are involved in a project from the beginning, you wind up with a stronger apartment.

The first floor was reordered into an entrance hall, a living room, a dining room, a library, and an expansive kitchen. The second floor contains the master bedroom, a playroom, and a bedroom for each child. The challenge for me was to tie all these rooms together. One of the ways I did so was with color.

I can just hear some people saying, "But her rooms are all white!" Let me explain that white happens to be a color. In fact, it's made up of all the colors in the spectrum. Or, as Donald Kaufman often says, there are ten thousand shades of white. White can be infused with

PREVIOUS SPREAD
I love symmetry, and you can certainly see it in the arrangement of furniture here. The swooping arms of the chairs in the foreground add a little nuance to the more regular shapes.

OPPOSITE
For these apartment owners, good fortune allowed them to purchase the floor above and gave them the opportunity to utilize the roof space to create this outdoor retreat. One simply can't do this in an urban area without the proper permissions and permits, which takes patience and understanding. But how wonderful that it was achieved. Dinner under the stars—how divine!

red or green or blue or yellow. The idea of a neutral background is not that it's color-less. It's just that the color is very sooth-ing. Most of my clients prefer neutrals like white and ivory and taupe and beige, find-ing them easy to live with. A red room can be very energizing, but you have to be up for it. Neutrals, on the other hand, are very calming. I can run them through the whole apartment, using the white in one room as the trim in another. Or perhaps the trim will be the same throughout the house and the wall color will change subtly. Or I might use the same color that's on the walls for the trim, but in a different finish. It will appear different because each finish—matte or eggshell or gloss—reflects the light differently. A neutral palette creates a pleasing continuity throughout a home.

In this living room, five Cy Twombly works on paper set the tone. At first, the clients thought they would hang a few on the wall above the fireplace and a few in the bedroom. But I thought it would be more dramatic to place them all in this one room, around the perimeter, so you could experi-ence them wherever you were sitting. I was thinking of the room at the Tate Modern in London filled with a series of paintings by Mark Rothko. There's an intriguing tension and a friendship between them. I thought the Twomblys would be even more powerful, as opposed to merely decorative, if they encircled the room.

Hanging art is a very particular skill. Even art consultants, who certainly know the value of a work of art, are often clueless when it comes to displaying it. I'm happy to direct anyone. I've spent decades

ABOVE

The very special Cy Twombly is a perfect pairing to the rich gray stone fireplace mantel, the perfect over-mantel solution.

OPPOSITE

The creamy paint on the walls in the living room provides a good backdrop for the art: the Twomblys are the stars, and the room is designed around them. French doors allow the light from the living room to spill into the foyer.

experimenting with all sorts of pieces, and by now I've developed a certain expertise.

One of the Twomblys was a slightly different size, so it made sense to give it the unique spot over the mantel. The mantel's gray stone almost seems to be part of the same palette. This was a coincidence. I do not believe in matching furnishings to art, or vice versa. When I was choosing the rug, I kept the grayish green tones of the Twomblys in mind, but I didn't try to duplicate them. When decorating a room, you don't match the art. You play to it.

The rug is a pale, relatively quiet Tabriz. Like the furniture, it doesn't upstage the art. The duplication of shapes—the paired armchairs, the twin club chairs balancing the sofa—sets up an agreeable symmetry. The pair of consoles on either side of the fireplace took forever to find. The furniture is all roughly the same height, low not high, which creates a uniformly low horizon line. This is a modernist trick. A traditional room would be more likely to have a tall secretary, various reading lamps, and a big old wing chair—which would make your eye move up and down. A low horizon line is easier on the eye and actually very restful.

I see a room in terms of geometry. A room is composed of planes. The ceiling is one plane. The furniture is another. The floor is a third. When I begin to design a room, I'm not thinking about how many fabrics I can fit in. I'm thinking about space—the way a wall turns, where a focal point could happen. I don't think I could ever begin with the decorating—shopping for little cachepots and trays and tassels. That part comes later, if at all.

The furniture in this room and the paint on the walls create a unified background for the art. The walls are the color of French vanilla ice cream—the good kind, with a lot of egg. The trim is another color—in the same tonal family but a little paler—and the ceiling is yet another.

I had the coffee table in the living room custom-made, with my favorite circles accenting the square. A collection of celadon glass adds a touch of fresh color, soft enough not to compete with the Cy Twombly drawings on the wall.

The doorway frames a dining room view that shows off the Ellsworth Kelly above the sideboard.

A 1940s Murano glass chandelier echoes the shape of the dining table. The colorful squares in the work by Ellsworth Kelly offer a nice counterpoint to all the pale curves.

Not white-white but tinted because I don't like bright white ceilings. And I never paint the walls and ceiling the same color. Never. I don't want to lose that plane. So this room, which many people would call white, is actually built up out of a lot of colors—the paint, the carpet, the Twomblys, the mantel. Every color is different yet similar, divided only by six degrees of separation. The closeness of the tones makes the room read as a whole. Sometimes I think it's harder to do this than a typical paint job, where you just pick out your favorite color and put it on the wall.

In the dining room, the clients wanted a round table because they felt it would be more conducive to conversation. I like a round table because I think it spins a square or rectangular room, adding a little movement. And then that graphic Ellsworth Kelly draws a long line across the wall and adds a little dash. The draperies are two shades darker than the walls. Why? Because if you're going for a blend, which I prefer, they can't be the exact same color. The dining chairs are upholstered in velvet in yet another shade. If your dining table is a big chunk of mahogany, make sure the dining chairs have a considerable amount of fabric on them. You want people to be comfortable enough to linger at the table after dinner and chat.

As soon as you walk into the library, you see this large window with a wonderful view of the city. It seemed logical to put the desk

In the library, a leather-wrapped desk by Jacques Adnet is positioned to take advantage of the view. You can rest a cup of coffee, or your feet, on the woven leather cubes.

there. It's a distinctive desk by Jacques Adnet, wrapped in leather and long enough that both husband and wife can share it. Then there's a big sofa opposite the fireplace, a chair to read in, and woven leather cubes to rest your feet on. What else do you need? A soft, thick carpet on the floor—a little lighter than the cocoa-painted walls.

The master bedroom is all about the bed, which is the only thing you really have to think about when you have this much space. All you need to do in this room is sleep. You don't need to worry about fitting in drawers and closets. Storage requirements can be taken care of in the dressing rooms and baths. The window in this bedroom was so large that we could fit it out with bookcases and a window seat. I could go from the bed to the window seat quite happily and never leave, so long as I had my favorite books on those shelves.

I think bedrooms should be as soft as possible. The carpet is thick and luxurious. The walls are upholstered in tone-on-tone leafy fabric—almost like soundproofing. It's so quiet in here, you know it's time to rest.

When I stay in a hotel, I study the bedroom to see what they've done to make it more comfortable. There's one basic architectural strategy that makes a big difference—an interior vestibule so that you're not right on the hall. That makes a hotel room feel more private and protected, and the same principle applies at home. I think passageways and connecting spaces between rooms really are a luxury. In this apartment, you pass through a vestibule with the dressing rooms before you get to the bed. When you come up the stairs from the first floor, you turn one way for the

ABOVE

A duvet always makes a bed look more inviting. Indeed, it's a hard choice between the bed and the window seat in this room. Both look so comfortable.

RIGHT

The upholstered walls make this room feel as cozy as a cocoon. Clean white cotton sheets and pillowcases are even more inviting when you spritz lavender oil in your ironing water. I like to read in bed, so I always make sure my clients have plenty of pillows for support. Notice I installed a reading light over the window seat as well.

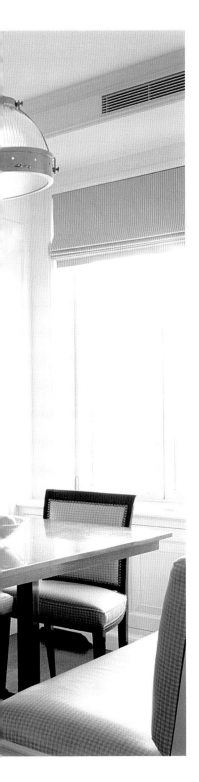

master bedroom suite and the other way for the children's rooms. That's a very sensible division of the space.

In the kitchen, the cabinetry was designed by the architect to the client's specifications. It is white and old-fashioned, with granite countertops. These days, I'd say 90 percent of the countertops we do are granite. It's one of the hardest, least porous stones, so there's less worry about stains once it's sealed. Marble is beautiful, but it does stain and you have to accept that. The worst, in my opinion, is concrete. It can create havoc, unless it's very well made and well sealed. Wood countertops seem to be gradually making their way back. Some people love the look of old-fashioned butcher block. Nobody wants tile—it's hard to dig crumbs out of the grout. I personally love stainless steel, but it scratches. You just have to look at the scratches as part of the patina.

I want a kitchen you can work in and live in, hopefully with room to eat a meal as well. Here, there's a large breakfast table with chairs on three sides. On the fourth, we built a banquette. We did that because this couple have three children. With plenty of playdates, you can always squeeze a few more friends onto a banquette.

An all-white kitchen always looks clean and fresh. An unusual cabinet, lit from within, hangs from the ceiling over the island and separates the cooking and breakfast areas.

4 | ELEGANT LIVING

hen you're searching for the perfect apartment in Manhattan, and one presents itself, you say, "Yes! I'll take it!" Quickly, before another buyer snatches it up.

This extraordinary corner apartment came with great views and beautiful details, which we decided to preserve. Some decorators can't wait to erase any trace of their predecessors, but my attitude is, Why get rid of something that works? The entryway was already paneled with lovely honey-colored wood, which made it feel warm and intimate and probably a little smaller than it actually was. But that's not necessarily a bad thing, as it created a shift in scale. When you move from the entryway to the living room, which is painted off-white, the living room feels larger than it actually is, because of the perception of moving from dark to light.

If you want to create some drama in an entryway, look to the walls and ceilings. Make something special out of them with moldings, paint, wallpaper, or wood. Here, the paneled walls and the coffered ceiling are like a drumroll, building up anticipation for the rest of the apartment. Usually there's not much room for furniture in an entryway, but we found two Danish Empire commodes that look as if they were made for the space. They fit perfectly on either side of the door to the living room, with an opaline

PREVIOUS SPREAD

The corner study is paneled in the same wood as the entryway, which creates an instant sense of warmth. Near the window, the English writing table's oval shape throws a curve into the room.

RIGHT

There's a distinctive 1930s look to all the lighting in this entryway, from the opaline glass lamps to the chandelier that centers the room and picks up the honey color of the paneling. Stepping off the elevator, you can look straight through the living room to the view of Central Park.

glass lamp from the 1930s on top of each commode. There's always something comforting about walking into a lamp-lit room. It's cozy. It makes me feel like I'm home.

There's a little lesson in the way you enter the living room. It's not the classic entrance from the middle or the end but off to one side. In order to make this work, the architect did something clever. The door aligns with a window on the opposite wall, so the first thing you see is the view of Central Park. If you're renovating, pay attention to these kinds of relationships. Sometimes, you get a much better layout simply by moving a door.

It made sense to me to create a focal point with the furniture as well. A custom-made card table was commissioned for the spot by the window. It's surrounded by four art deco chairs and creates another center of activity. There are actually three seating areas in this living room—an intimate group by the fireplace, where one or two people would feel comfortable; another group anchored by a sofa against a wall for a larger party; and a third around the card table. What pulls them all together is the rug. A rug is a field of color and texture and pattern on which you're going to play. I generally keep the furniture on the carpet. It's the ground. It binds the whole room together. At first you might think it's the only color and pattern in the room, but look more closely. All the furniture may be upholstered in shades of ivory and cream and white, but each fabric has a different texture and pattern. There's a tone-on-tone damask and a stripe. I love those big fat tufted chairs to the right of the fireplace—they're like little clouds that have come down from the sky. Then there are

OPPOSITE

Another great coffee table, made of twisted glass, anchors a second seating area. The card table by the window is ready for an afternoon game of bridge. Notice the patterned fabric placed just on the back of the chairs for effect.

OVERLEAF

A pair of mirrors captures more light. Sconces on all the walls avoid cluttering the room with lamps.

various wood-framed chairs—I believe in edges—to keep it all from floating away.

That elegant ribbon frieze, done in plaster at the cornice line, was already there, and we just accented it with white paint. But the fireplace didn't have a surround, so I designed a simple one in limestone. Then I set a circle on top. It's something I made out of wood, lacquered white. I think of it as an art object. A circle is so pure. It's even better than a square because it never stops. This one is just propped on the mantel without a stand because I like it better that way. And now I have a circle to balance all those squares—the fireplace and the two mirrors. The opaline glass sconces offer an interesting contrast. They're kind of lacy. It's rare to find six antique sconces that match, and I used them all around the room so they create a rhythm and add a soft glow. The furnishings are quiet, calm, and understated.

The paneling from the entryway is repeated in the corner study. I chose a taupe chenille for the upholstery, neutral and soft to the touch. The curtains are another shade of taupe, and then the rug brings in yet another. If you're going to do a monochromatic scheme, you want to change the value of the color so it subtly shifts from lighter to darker. You layer the tones, which is much more interesting than making everything exactly the same shade.

In the dining room, the walls were already covered in squares of parchment that was too pretty to remove. The dining table is a new, extendable version of a French original. The beauty of the French art deco chairs is in their simplicity. They have a delicate profile, outlined in mahogany, with enough upholstery to make them comfortable. An

OPPOSITE

I like to use glass chandeliers because they don't encumber a space. (You can see right through them.) The sideboard is French, and the oval shape echoes the table. There are no hard edges, just graceful curves.

OVERLEAF

Because the window in the dining room is off center, I treated it very simply so it doesn't throw the room off balance. The curtain fabric is light enough so the sunshine still comes through.

elegant dining chair that is also comfortable is a rare find. The glass chandelier is French as well, with graceful lines. A chandelier does not have to have lots of dangling baubles to be beautiful, and this proves it.

The master bedroom has upholstered silk walls and draperies, but it's hard to focus on anything but the bed. I had it custom made, based on a French 1930s original by Jules Leleu. It's upholstered in white cashmere, accented with silk rosettes, in a lovely channeled design. It's also incredibly comfortable—Proust could have written his novels in this bed. Once you get in, you never want to get out. The bedside tables were also custom made, with a drawer and a shelf for books.

There were two recesses in the wall that needed something special, so I had two chocolate lacquered chests of drawers made in England to fit. Then I hung two beautiful mirrors over them to capture the light from the two windows and reflect it back. In an apartment, which always seems to have more enclosed spaces than a house, you need to be very careful about window treatments. I like to keep curtains simple so they don't block the natural light. It's unusual for me to even do a valance, but I made an exception here. The room is so tall, and the windows just seemed to require that crowning touch. Wall-to-wall carpeting, thick and luxurious, covers the floor and completes that feeling of being cocooned in softness. Who wouldn't want to lie down in that gorgeous bed and end the day here?

OPPOSITE

The corner holds matching his-and-hers reading chairs. The curtains are made of silk. To upholster the walls, we stretched more silk over individual panels. Wood moldings mask the corner seams.

OVERLEAF

The Calla bed, modeled on an original by Jules Leleu, is one of my designs for Hickory Chair. Here, we upholstered it in cashmere. Softness is the subtext of this room, and we carried it through on almost every surface with silk-covered walls and wall-to-wall carpeting. The door on the left leads to the dressing rooms and baths.

It's useless to try to make a collector stop. Some people are simply entranced by beautiful things, so when they find something they like, they just naturally want to possess it. These clients are connoisseurs. Over the years, they have amassed an extraordinary trove of paintings, drawings, photographs, and other decorative objects. They are committed, informed, and infinitely patient—always willing to wait for just the right item. As a result, their collection represents the best of the best. So when they found this apartment, there was no need to think about adding moldings or paneling or cornices. Complex architectural embellishments were utterly unnecessary here because the rooms take a backseat. Art is the first note played.

It's apparent as soon as you step off the elevator and approach the front door. On one side, there's a table made of elaborately cut and curled metal, with a marble top. It was designed in the 1930s by the French master Jules Leleu. Above it hangs a mirror from the same period, rimmed in cobalt blue. This was an exhilarating moment in design, when Leleu and Jean-Michel Frank and Pierre Chareau were all working at the height of their powers. Paris was a design mecca, full of busy little ateliers where artisans were creating one-of-a-kind objects like this, mostly on special order for discerning clients. It was a transitional period, when the elaborate fancies of Victoriana and art nouveau were giving way to the sleeker, angular lines of art deco and streamline moderne. Artists were inspired by the

PREVIOUS SPREAD
Most people would have arranged these photographs in the foyer in a continuous row. Instead, they are broken up to create an interesting asymmetry. The Émile-Jacques Ruhlmann chair next to the console table is part of the dining room set.

OPPOSITE
In the elevator vestibule, the pièce de résistance is a console table by Jules Leleu. Its stylized metal curlicues represent a high point of art deco style. An opaline glass dish light casts a soft glow on the creamy yellow walls.

ABOVE

That spectacular vase with its matching stand makes me think of the Vienna Secessionists and the Wiener Werkstätte, and demonstrates how one piece can hold a wall. If you want to make a ceiling feel higher, look for vertically striped wallpaper and a low chair rail.

OVERLEAF

Choosing a rug for this living room was a challenge. A solid cream carpet would have been too bland. An Oriental would have been too busy. Finally we settled on this handwoven cotton rug by Elizabeth Eakins, which adds just the right amount of structure and complexity. The soft, subtle colors blend in without drawing too much attention. Of course, the architect in me loves this rug for its grid.

promise of the machine age. It was the beginning of modernism.

Boundaries between fields were dissolving as artists designed furniture and designers made singular pieces of furniture that were more like works of art. Inside the apartment, in the entrance foyer, the rug on the floor was designed by Diego Giacometti. My clients found it, and I love the strong graphic shapes and the simple linear design. The floor is limestone and the rug is almost the same color, which makes the black in the pattern stand out all the more. I bought the console table in Paris, and I'm guessing that it was made by Pierre Chareau. There's an amazing delicacy to the iron fronds, which curl out so gracefully at the tips to support the marble top. It's a unique, sculptural piece that holds the whole wall.

We decided to keep the existing chair rail, which is quite low and makes the ceiling feel that much higher. Below it, the wall is painted. For the space above it, I chose a striped wallpaper—tone on tone, so it adds a little texture to the background while still remaining neutral. A chair rail would have been common in apartments of the period when the furniture was made, so it provides a certain context. And then the wallpaper adds a little eccentricity. The space is not a pure white gallery; it's a home.

You can see that very clearly in the living room. It's all about living artfully, but that doesn't mean you have to sacrifice comfort for art. There are two comfortable sofas, one from the 1940s with a matching easy chair. Then there are two charming Leleu chairs, upholstered in a period pink-and-white pattern. They can come forward or backward to suit the size of the group. I always like to have a few chairs in the

mix that can move around. The coffee table is also French, from the 1930s. Do you see how the legs wrap the corners, eliminating the sharp edges? That makes it easier to walk around—less danger of bumping into it.

For the fireplace, I designed a simple stone surround in the style of Jean-Michel Frank. The wrought iron fire screen is by Leleu, and the floor lamp nearby is in the same vein, although it was done much later. Just look at those marvelous curves on the lamp base. I've never seen another like it. That's a little sculpture right there. It's fun to search out these pieces at auctions, in galleries, and at antiques shops. In Europe, I might stop off to see an old church on the way to meet a dealer and rummage through his basement. My clients also love the thrill of the hunt, and they shared in my pleasure over the pieces I discovered.

ABOVE

I found an unusual pomegranate pink fabric for the Jules Leleu chair, which looks as if it could have been made during the same period. The wrought iron fire screen is another Leleu piece. When I saw that floor lamp with the intricate metal base, I thought they went well together.

OPPOSITE

The rich green upholstery amplifies the color of the Skyscraper bookcase filled with the owner's collection of wood, ceramic, and pottery objects.

OVERLEAF LEFT

Any surface becomes an opportunity for a composition. Émile-Jacques Ruhlmann designed this silver coffee service with ivory handles. It looks almost like a sculpture itself, set off by the dark wood of the cabinet.

OVERLEAF RIGHT

The console table, made of stone and iron, is a contemporary piece but also manages to suggest the art deco period. The small bronze figures on the table echo the large figure in the painting above.

I think most people who love beautiful things have a vision about how they want their house to look, but they can't quite execute it. That's where a decorator comes in to act as maestro and make a disparate group of objects come together like a piece of music. There should be crescendos, and moments of quietness, in the scheme. Decorating is about color, texture, shape, proportion, and balance. But balance, for example, is not as simple as merely pairing things up. Consider that large painting on the living room wall just left of the door to the dining room. There had to be something of equal weight and interest on the other side. Most people would have looked for another painting, but I chose something completely different—a Skyscraper cabinet designed in the 1920s by Paul Frankl, a Viennese designer who immigrated to New York City and helped define the look of American modernism. This is one of his iconic pieces, an early example of

RIGHT

When a dining table is not in use, it provides the perfect place to showcase your favorite silver. These pieces all share a Ruhlmann-esque aesthetic. I think the double-height candlesticks are exquisite.

OVERLEAF

The mirrored wall between the windows in the dining room makes the space feel twice as large. It's unusual to hang mirror on top of mirror, but it works. I love how the oval mirror, designed by Ruhlmann, frames the reflection of the painting in the opposite room. The chandelier is a fine Wiener Werkstätte piece that could have adorned a Vienna coffee shop in another era.

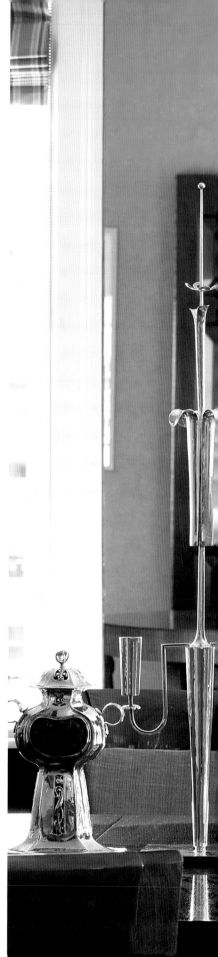

ABOVE

This is a working library, with his-and-hers desks, books and papers piled everywhere, and photographs propped on the floor. Not every room has to be neat and pristine. If things aren't orderly, I can't think. But other people think differently.

OPPOSITE

The window shade and matching bedcover add softness in a bedroom of modern, stylized furniture.

his Skyscraper series. He would pick up some scrap wood in his workroom and make something out of it. That's not just a furniture maker. That's an artist.

This apartment is full of historic pieces, but they're not treated reverently. Instead, they are used every day. Émile-Jacques Ruhlmann, one of the masters of art deco, designed the dining room table and chairs. They're worthy of a museum, but there's nothing museum-like and stiff about this dining room. The walls had been painted a warm salmon shade. The clients liked the color, so we decided to keep it. The window wall was mirrored, and they decided to keep that, too, because it opened up the room. Then my client found an oval mirror, also by Ruhlmann, and we had to decide where to put it. We did something unusual and hung it right on top of the mirrored wall. So you have mirror upon mirror, which creates an interesting conundrum. The reflections fracture and duplicate. It's a little mysterious. When you first walk into the room, you can't quite figure out what is going on. It's a moment of wonder. The mirror wouldn't have been half as memorable if we had just hung it normally on a plain wall.

I love the eccentricity of their collection—the Ruhlmann table, the Skyscraper cabinet, the Leleu chairs. They bought each piece because they felt passionate about it, not because they needed it or thought it would be a good investment. They saw it and they loved it. That's what collecting is all about—the relationship between you and the object. It should give you pleasure. Everything in this apartment gives these clients such joy.

I f it were possible to x-ray an apartment, this one would prove to have very good bones. The ceilings are high and the proportions are grand. All of the principal rooms overlook Fifth Avenue and have the quintessential New York Central Park view. But the truly unique feature is the enormously large entrance hall—forty feet long by sixteen feet wide—although in this case it functions as more of an entrance gallery. Paintings by William Baziotes, Barnett Newman, and Franz Kline hang on the walls. As soon as you walk in, you're bowled over by the art. It's tempting to stop and sit down on one of the slim, streamlined Italian sofas and simply contemplate the blur of color and shape on the canvases. The two sofas are the only furniture in the room, which has the stillness and poise of a gallery.

One of the reasons the apartment works so beautifully is that the architecture is on the same scale as the art. Architect Boris Baranovich took the doors all the way up to the ceiling and increased their width. The proportions of the room are very pleasing to the eye. The hall is the spine of the apartment, connecting the various wings. French doors, with panels made of glass to let in the light, lead to the living room, where there's a Mark Rothko between the windows, another Kline over the fireplace, and a Philip Guston and an Arshile Gorky on one wall. When you have good art, you don't want to do anything too fussy. I hate those apartments where you can't see the paintings in between all the pillows and fabrics and flowers.

PREVIOUS SPREAD

If you own large-scale art, you need plenty of space in order to see it properly. That is one of the laws of decorating physics. Fortunately, this entrance hall is big enough to let the paintings breathe, and the limestone floor provides a suitably neutral base.

OPPOSITE

Wall space for the art collector is always a premium. An opportunity is presented to hang a favorite black-and-white painting over a sofa and chairs on the way to the library.

Everything here is as clean as possible. The fireplace is pure, just a rectangle made out of limestone. There are no elaborate moldings, just a fine line of trim around the doors. I deliberately kept all the furnishings at the same height, which creates a low horizon line that feels very serene and doesn't interfere with the art. There are two seating areas, one at the fireplace and one on the opposite wall. If I couldn't find exactly the kind of furniture I envisioned, I designed it myself, in a 1960s idiom that just seemed to work with all the 1950s and 1960s abstract expressionist art. I had the two matching sofas in front of the fireplace custom made. That long, unbroken line of the seat cushion feels very 1960s to me. The long, lean upholstered bench is by Florence Knoll, one of the great designers of the era. Pieces that have that kind of age and character are hard to find. I had to scout around. In a room that is this refined, everything you put in it has to sing.

That Florence Knoll bench is so chic. I placed it perpendicular to the pair of sofas and parallel to a third sofa against the wall. I like how all the pieces form these interlocking planes. That's what gives the room dynamism. It's almost like the brushstrokes in the paintings. I do think traditional American furniture looks great with contemporary art, and I will keep on combining different periods. But I have to say that modern 1960s furniture really suits modern 1960s art. These pieces—both furniture and art—are bigger, bolder. They demand your attention. And they have a simplicity that is very powerful. The clients

The living room has two large windows and three doorways. In order to make room for all those circulation paths, the furniture had to come off the walls. Frankly, I just think furniture looks better when you float it in the middle of a room. Here, we created two main seating groups.

asked for calm and continuity. I strived to make the apartment feel as seamless as one of Donald Judd's sculptures.

Most of the fabrics are neutrals. I took the colors I used on the fabrics and matched them to the yarns that were used to weave the custom carpet. So it's actually made up of five different shades. You're not quite sure just what color it is. It isn't gray and it isn't beige. Because of the strength and energy of the art on the walls, I knew the room needed a plain carpet. I wanted it to be neutral, without being boring. If something is this complex, it seems a little inadequate to call it neutral, doesn't it? We had to order several three-foot samples before we got exactly the right shade. The carpet had to work with the color of the wood on the doors and the floor. It has the effect of pulling the whole room together. It marries all the various pieces in a subtle way.

Subtlety is hard to do. Very hard. It's like finding the right note in a piece of music. The carpet strikes a chord. I didn't want it to look muddy, and I didn't want it to look dull. It's made up of neutrals that balance one another out, in a way. Sometimes I think it would be easier to choose a few bright colors and call it quits. Or just blue and white. Pick out three blue-and-white fabrics, paint the walls white, and you're done.

This, on the other hand, requires a more complex kind of orchestration, a blend of color and shape and texture that looks effortless, although it's anything but. It helps when the architect appreciates subtlety and has given you the best possible shell. For example, here's one very clever thing that Baranovich did. He kept all the doors near the windows, so you can always see the full run of windows and therefore borrow the space and the light. It creates a lovely arrangement of rooms—another axis that draws your eye to the farthest point, which has the effect of making the apartment seem even larger. The curtains

Large windows tend to extend the experience of a space to the exterior skyscape. Rather than feeling confined by the walls, you have a feeling of expansiveness—another benefit of a room with a view. Why obscure it by overdressing the windows? And with a Mark Rothko painting in between, I certainly didn't want the curtains to compete.

are just a wisp of sheer fabric, nothing more. They blend into the walls. All the windows are treated the same, so when you look through a door into an adjoining room, you get the impression that the windows go on forever. Of course, we also created pockets for solar screens, to protect the paintings from too much sun.

One of the first things I think about in a room is light—in which direction does the room face? Does it get enough sun? And how should I light it at night? The two standing lamps on either side of the living room fireplace are not accidental. I really do believe that you have to have light at eye level. Lamp lighting is more elegant than a cluster of recessed lights on a ceiling, and much more flattering. I am also very careful not to overlight the art. All those little brass fixtures

ABOVE

A delightfully large-scale painting of a flower bouquet animates the simplicity and utilitarian aspect of this generously sized kitchen and breakfast room. If you love art, don't be afraid to hang it at will!

OPPOSITE

In this dining room, two square tables offer more flexibility than one large rectangular table. They can be placed together, as seen here, or moved apart to accommodate different numbers of guests. The simplicity of the tables is echoed in the pure lines of the china, silver, and glassware.

over paintings can look cluttered, and they feel a little pretentious to me. You don't light art to show it off. You just want to make sure you can see it properly.

In the dining room, we hung a painting from the clients' collection and made it the focal point. They wanted to be able to seat ten or twelve for dinner. I couldn't find a table I liked that was long enough, so I had two made—very pure, very plain. Two squares that butt together or can be pulled apart, so my clients can vary the seating arrangement. Instead of a predictable chandelier, I had a different kind of light fixture made. It looks like a modern version of something you might have found over a billiard table. Three shades rather than two, as you might expect since there are two tables. But that irregular relationship creates an interesting moment. I also had the dining chairs made, and they're the closest I could get to a Donald Judd. Just a straight wooden chair, with an upholstered back and seat so they're not uncomfortable.

This kind of subtlety needs a few surprises, otherwise it risks becoming bland. The surprise in the master bedroom is the bench at the end of the bed. It's made out of stainless steel, with a soft upholstered top. The steel adds a little sheen and breaks up the solidity of the bed. I love that tall chunky headboard, upholstered in a wheat-colored linen. When you have a room like this, all in the same shades of one warm color, you're enveloped in peace. The night table is a little composition in itself—a crisp, clean mahogany box with leather-wrapped drawers, designed by another master of modernism, George Nelson. I don't subscribe to the theory that a bedside table needs to have a lot of stuff on it. These surfaces are too pure to clutter them up. Look at those beautiful brass pulls. Mies van der Rohe was right: God is in the details.

Bedrooms, for me, are all about the bed. Here, the height of the mattress and the headboard is a little exaggerated to emphasize its importance. I like the contrast of that vertical picture above the horizontal chest of drawers.

When I see something I like, I know it. I was looking for a new apartment, and as soon as I walked into this space, I fell in love. Sliding shoji screens blocked the light from the windows and faded grass cloth covered the walls, but I was already stripping it off and knocking down walls in my head. I knew exactly what I wanted to do with the space—here's where I'll entertain, that's where I'll dine, there's where I'll read.

I already had the new layout in my head when I called my friend Mark Simon, an architect with whom I've collaborated many times, to help execute it. Together, we took the apartment apart and rebuilt it, deftly working around certain existing conditions like the location of the elevator shafts, the back stairs, and the plumbing risers. If you're renovating, I say, bite the bullet and do it all in one fell swoop. You'll save yourself the trouble of multiple smaller fix-ups later that will interfere with your life.

There were built-in cabinets on either side of the fireplace, and I took them out because I wanted to widen the living room. Now there are niches on either side, which serve to expand the space visually. I didn't want an elaborate mantel. One day Mark just drew that virtual

PREVIOUS SPREAD
The large mirror over the dining table extends the room and reflects the windows. But what really determines the mood is that lovely curved sofa, in lieu of the typical dining chairs. A sofa by a dining table indicates that this room is more casual, intimate, and unexpected; it's an invitation to relax.

OPPOSITE
When I renovated this apartment I ordered new soundproof windows, with black mullions instead of white. Black is my accent color throughout the apartment—notice the almost black lampshades (lined with gold paper to cast a warm light). The black mullions add a bit of architecture, and at night they disappear.

OVERLEAF
The fireplace wall in my living room hides the flues for the whole building, so the depth was a given. But why bring it out even farther into the room by adding a mantel? There was something very powerful about that flat plane, so we simply incised a few lines into the wall to create a much more unusual and intriguing virtual mantel.

mantel on the wall, and it completely captivated me. A few abstract lines incised into the plaster had such impact. It's a witty illusion. In a sense, the whole wall becomes the fireplace. The wall goes straight to the floor. No baseboard. I painted it a different color than the rest of the room. I know, the whole room is white. But the fireplace is a different shade of white. Donald Kaufman mixed up a light coffee color for me and painted a sample stretch of the wall. We took a look and shook our heads. Then he mixed up an extra-light coffee and we nodded.

The rest of the walls are painted Donald Kaufman number 51, one of my favorite whites. I want to say it's pure, but can a white still be pure if it has every other color in it? Donald puts all these different pigments into his paint. That's why I like it. It changes with the light, and yet it is always calm. Like fashion people who work with color all day long, I want to come home to a blank slate at night. In the most practical sense, white also makes the apartment seem as big as possible.

White is my mainstay. White is my solace. Naturally, my chairs and sofa are upholstered in white. The sofa belonged to Syrie Maugham, one of England's legendary decorators. How appropriate that I should own a sofa that used to be hers because she, too, was famous for her white rooms. I resisted having it re-covered for so long but finally had to succumb because the silk was shredding. The beauty of the sofa is the way the cushion wraps around the arm, and the tufting—punctuated with little silk rosettes. It's a very distinctive piece and so long that it didn't fit in the elevator. We had to hoist it up through the window. Actually, the sofa in the dining room had to come in that way, too. It's upholstered in a very pale yellow because that's the way it was when I found it, and it hasn't worn out yet. I don't really like new things.

I can seat ten in this room, if I pull over the chairs from the dining table. The furniture arrangement is a bit unusual. There's an English library table behind the Syrie Maugham sofa, with a long English Regency bench. It's covered in a gauffrage velvet that's shredding, as well. The table gives me a place to put the lamp and another spot to seat people during a dinner party. The coffee table is one of my

ABOVE

I extended the fireplace wall to create an unobtrusive nook for books and firewood. The Micah Lexier artwork over the fireplace is made of very thin stainless steel. Some people think it looks like a scribble. Others see it as a puff of smoke.

RIGHT

The English library table behind the sofa has a distinctive stretcher bar with a little roundel at the end—very pretty. I paired it with an English Regency bench. They give me another place to seat people during a dinner party, and another surface where I can display a few favorite things. I've run out of wall space, so now I'm buying objects—such as that thick glass sculpture by Bernard Dejonghe and the simple black cubes.

OVERLEAF

I took down the wall between the living room and the dining alcove, which makes the apartment feel much bigger. Now you can see all three windows at once. I'm so in love with white. The curtains are white, just like the walls. Even most of the art in here is white. Other colors go in other rooms. The large-scale photograph over the console table is by Seton Smith.

serendipitous finds. I saw it at an auction house and said, "That's my table." It was designed in the 1950s by Paul McCobb, and it has the clarity of a mathematical equation, with a lower shelf and one asymmetrical drawer. The top is covered in mottled leather. The coffee table is a slim rectangle, and then the two-tiered tables flanking the fireplace are squares. Of course, they're actually étagères, meant to display various objects, but I keep them almost bare. I prefer to see the light through them. I am enthralled with negative space. I just want to see their shape. I've had books on them, but I always end up taking them off. For the moment, the tables stay empty.

There used to be a wall between the living room and the dining alcove. That's gone now. You can see the difference in the pattern of the floorboards, if you want to look, but things like that don't bother me. It's just another kind of geometry. I put the curved sofa against the side wall, behind the dining table. I like a sofa or a banquette by a table because it's softer than a row of chairs and can hold more people in a pinch. I purchased the table from the Duke and Duchess of Windsor sale. It was their breakfast table. I spotted it at Sotheby's and decided I had to have it.

LEFT

One of these days, I'm going to have a big country kitchen with a great big slab of wood for a table—but not in Manhattan! I just don't have the room. This kitchen was designed to do everything I need very efficiently in a tight space: refrigerator drawers, pantry, and china storage on the left; sink and cooktop on the right. Glass doors at either end mean I can close off the kitchen without it feeling like a box.

OPPOSITE

A long hall connecting the front and back halves of the apartment became a gallery, where I hung my Donald Judd engravings. In a corridor, you need something to occupy the eye. Notice how the pedestal table is centered on the hallway. If you have a strong axis, you might as well play to it.

I hung a large mirror in the dining alcove to double the space and reflect the light from the windows. I believe in mirrors. When I start a job, I'm immediately walking through the rooms and calculating how many mirrors I can use. I have a mirror in my foyer, a pair in the living room, a mirror in the powder room . . . the list goes on and on.

But even the most beautiful mirror is of no use if the basic layout of the room is wrong. There was one aspect of this apartment that gave me pause—the kitchen. Its location—straight ahead as you walk through the front door—was less than ideal, and it was designed as a narrow galley. The space was already tight, and one wall was interrupted

ABOVE
From the library, a doorway opens to the master bath, which also connects to the master bedroom on another side. A floating counter holds the sink, and with a bench underneath (neatly covered in a shirred flannel skirt), it doubles as a dressing table.

OPPOSITE
This is my mini-library. I shipped the Gothic bookcase from London and then had the waist-high bookcases built to hold all my oversize art books. Each cube is 22 x 13 x 11 inches, which allows me to stack the books either vertically or horizontally.

by an awkward column that could not be moved. So I had to work around it. I pushed the wall out a foot to grab some more width. Then I paneled the column and built floor-to-ceiling cupboards next to it, to absorb it unobtrusively into the room. With all this new storage, I no longer needed upper cabinets on the other side. If you want to make a kitchen feel more spacious, consider replacing upper cabinets with open shelves, or removing them entirely. Getting rid of mine opened up the room, and suddenly I had the wall space to hang a favorite watercolor by Carolyn Brady. The last thing I wanted to do was move a bulky refrigerator into this newly pared-down room. Instead, I chose side-by-side refrigerator and freezer drawers that tuck under the countertop. The result: a compact, efficient kitchen that does not feel cramped, and when I like, I can close it off with glass-paneled pocket doors.

The kitchen had to stay in the traffic flow because it's part of the public space. To me, the front of an apartment is where you entertain and the back is where you live. The two halves of this apartment are separated by a long corridor, which gives it an unusual dumbbell shape. What can you do with a long hallway? I turned mine into a gallery and hung sixteen works on paper by Donald Judd. I'll bet you're not surprised. If you've read this far, you know not to expect botanicals from me. I wanted to get them all into the same space for impact, and they fit perfectly into the hall. The fact that they all portray rectangles is part of their fascination for me. I am continually struck by the power of simple shapes and the beauty of geometry.

The hallway used to lead to a warren of little rooms, but I cleared all that out to make a master suite, with a study that doubles as a guest room. On the way into the suite, you pass through a library area with built-in bookcases. Initially, I thought I could accommodate all my books in the office or at my home in the country, but that was a futile hope. No matter how hard I try to be restrained, I just can't resist a beautiful new art book, and the volumes keep accumulating. When I gave up my London apartment, I couldn't give up my beloved furniture, so I shipped it all home and put the Gothic bookcase here. I had to shave three inches off the base to get it in. It, too, is already full. No matter. I love to live with my books. Sometimes I feel they're all the decoration a room needs.

My bedroom is not large, but since the pocket doors to the study are usually open, it feels twice as big. It does have one large window, and I hung the tattersall silk curtains all the way across the wall to give the impression that the window is even larger than it actually is. The Calla bed is my own design, and it is part of my collection for Hickory Chair. It has a lovely upholstered headboard, which you can hardly see for all the pillows. At night, I pile the ones I don't use on that slipper chair. That's part of my practical streak. If you're going to have a lot of decorative pillows, you must have a convenient place to put them while you sleep, and that does not mean the floor. My bedside tables are chests of drawers, which I need

TOP

In my apartment I chose not to put a TV across from the bed, but instead a large watercolor of a white iris. Double pocket doors visually enlarge the room into the study.

ABOVE

Here, I chose to include a TV, paper supplies, and a file behind doors in my study.

OPPOSITE

The story about my entryway is that there is no entryway—just room enough to open the door and then you're immediately in the apartment. But I created the impression of an entryway with that mirror and the slim Chinese console table that just fits into the recessed wall. I made the hanging light fixture from an old measuring scale by unhooking the pan and having it wired to hold a light.

OVERLEAF

A painting by Yuko Shiraishi hangs over my bed. It's actually made up of five separate pieces, and together they form a line. The colors are deep and rich, but it's the purity of that line that got me. The curtains are made of a brown-and-cream silk tattersall, and the slipper chair is covered in a beige-and-white check. If you've read this far, you should know not to expect fabrics with flowers in my bedroom!

for extra storage. Maybe because I do what I do, I always find myself organizing and reorganizing my possessions. I believe in keeping most everything inside drawers or behind doors, if you can manage to live that way.

But there are exceptions to the rule. Some things I like to keep in view—my art, my books, and certain talismans. When you walk into the apartment, your eye automatically goes to an unusual pedestal table with an octagonal top (more geometry!). In the center of it is a round tray that holds a collection of tortoiseshell objects. They're all gathered together because they look neater and have more impact that way. These antique tortoiseshell card cases and cigarette cases and matchbox holders are very special to me, because they used to belong to Alexander Breckenridge, who was my professor at the New York School of Interior Design. He was a scholar and a gentleman who presented me with beautiful books and taught me about taste. I grew up in a little town in Michigan, and my knowledge of the decorative arts was still spotty when I arrived in New York. Alexander introduced me to a way of seeing. He taught me to appreciate art and beauty, whether in the curve of a chair leg or the forms of a sculpture. It gives me great pleasure to walk into my house every day and see the objects he loved.

A working desk space does not always require a computer. I prefer a collection of favorite objects and a legal pad in the top drawer.

CLASSICAL REFINEMENT

There is something so rich and intimate about a room paneled in dark wood. It is not so unusual to choose it for a library, but these clients had something bigger in mind. They wanted a living room paneled in mahogany.

They were not concerned that it would be too dark, because the room has generous windows and two French doors that open onto a long terrace. It is washed in sunlight during the day, so we could afford to cultivate a few shadows. Peter Cook was the architect on this project, and he designed the paneling, which started out looking a lot more Tudor. But it is hard to hang art on very complicated paneling, so we ended up going for a more classic look. Now there's a large panel over the sofa with narrow panels on each side. In the center, we hung a painting by Michael Gregory that portrays rays of sun bursting through clouds in an evening sky, or is it a sunrise? It doesn't really matter which, because the painting is about light and dark and so is the room.

With all that wood on the walls we couldn't do more wood on the floor, so the living room is carpeted wall-to-wall in a lovely shade of cream. The carpet creates a cool neutral platform that shows off the lines of the tufted English chairs and the scrolled legs of the side table. The sofa is one that I have designed, with English country house proportions. It has a deep, deep seat—notice the pitch of the back. You're meant to sink into this sofa, rather than sit straight up at attention.

Lighting is crucial to the mood of a room. The paneling may be dark, but that doesn't mean you should spoil the effect by overlighting

PREVIOUS SPREAD

The apartment originally had ordinary white walls like so many others. Architect Peter Cook added the mahogany paneling to make it feel much more luxurious. And because the beautiful wood detailing around the windows makes curtains seem redundant, I decided recessed shades were all that was needed.

OPPOSITE

A unique feature of this particular apartment is a custom-designed clear-glass-and-metal front door. As no other tenant shares the elevator foyer, this is easily allowable.

it. I knew I didn't want to break up the ceiling with light fixtures, because a ceiling usually looks much more beautiful without them. I prefer to see a smooth, white plane. I also didn't like the idea of a lot of little lamps, so instead I lit the room with hurricane sconces. They create a nice glow against the mahogany. I found a long English library table to set near the window, which was the logical place for it. It always makes sense to put a writing table near the light. The chair beside it is English Regency, inlaid with ivory.

The living room opens into the dining room, which we turned into an informal eating area with an open kitchen. I find that people have less and less use for formal dining rooms these days. Unless you eat dinner in there every night or give frequent dinner parties, the room is rarely used. It makes no sense to waste space, especially in

OPPOSITE

We enlarged the doorway between the living room and the kitchen to create the impression of more space. A sofalike banquette creates an informal and very comfortable dining area in the kitchen. Mahogany moldings accent the ceiling and tie the room together.

ABOVE

At first glance, this doesn't even look like a kitchen, until you notice the faucet against the back wall. The island is equipped with refrigerator drawers, and the range is recessed into the wall to make it more unobtrusive.

an apartment, where it is usually at a premium. So my advice is, make the dining room do double duty as a study or a library, or jettison it entirely. These clients did not want to dedicate a whole room to dining. All they wanted was a larger kitchen with a table where they could sit in the morning and have breakfast, or settle in to make phone calls during the day. I found a nineteenth-century English pedestal table that was just the right size. Instead of dining chairs, I designed a very comfortable banquette that could be mistaken for a sofa—that's how cozy it looks—and had it upholstered in the same cream that I used in the living room.

The kitchen itself is practically invisible. There are no upper cabinets to give it away. The island and the lower cupboards are all made of mahogany, which relates to the living room and has the same elegant quality. It's a very discreet kitchen, in a very refined room.

The apartment has a second floor, and when you go up the stairs you arrive at a spacious hallway, which leads to the master suite. The four-poster bed was made in England to my design, based on an English Regency original. The mahogany headboard is exceptionally high. The canopy is shirred and so is the bed skirt, which dresses it up a bit. True to form, the rest of the furniture in the room is English. There's a chaise for reading, upholstered in the same creamy fabric as the little sofa at the foot of

ABOVE
A maid's room adjacent to the kitchen was reconceived as a butler's pantry and outfitted with a large farmhouse sink.

OPPOSITE
Pull-out drawers in a cabinet are lined in dark green felt and fitted for china and wine storage.

OVERLEAF
At the top of the stairs leading to the bedroom floor, there was enough space in the hall to create a little seating area. French doors open to a large bathroom designed for the wife.

LEFT

When a four-poster bed dominates a bedroom, I like
to soften its mass with a shirred valance and dust ruffle.

ABOVE

A glimpse of the master bedroom is reflected in
a nineteenth-century French églomisé mirror.

OVERLEAF

Mirrored inserts on the mahogany doors in the
dressing room reflect a makeup table.

CLASSICAL REFINEMENT

145

the bed. We actually managed to fit in quite a lot of furniture, but the room doesn't feel crammed. There's a nice balance between feminine curves and straight edges. The tall mahogany book-case represents the more masculine contingent. But I'll let you in on a secret. The books behind the grillwork are actually just bindings, and the cabinet hides a TV.

The his-and-hers baths and dressing rooms are as beautifully appointed as those in a fine old English hotel. Her rooms are painted a lovely shade of cream, and his are paneled in—what else?—mahogany. Dark wood is the theme carried through the whole apartment, and it looks even richer against all the light cream colors in the upholstery and on the walls. The dark and the light balance each other out, and that contrast creates a strength that neither would have alone. It's a classic combination that makes for a handsome home.

ABOVE

In the husband's bathroom, a glass door opens to a marble shower with a matching marble bench. Because it's a stream shower, he needed a place to sit. We built another seat into the mahogany millwork, which makes this bath feel more like an actual room. The effect is very luxurious.

OPPOSITE

In the wife's bathroom, the tub is recessed into an arched niche accented with marble columns on either side. Cove lighting casts a gentle glow. You know how much I love furniture in a bathroom. This little stool can hold a cell phone, a drink, a book. The mosaic floor is decorated with a leafy border.

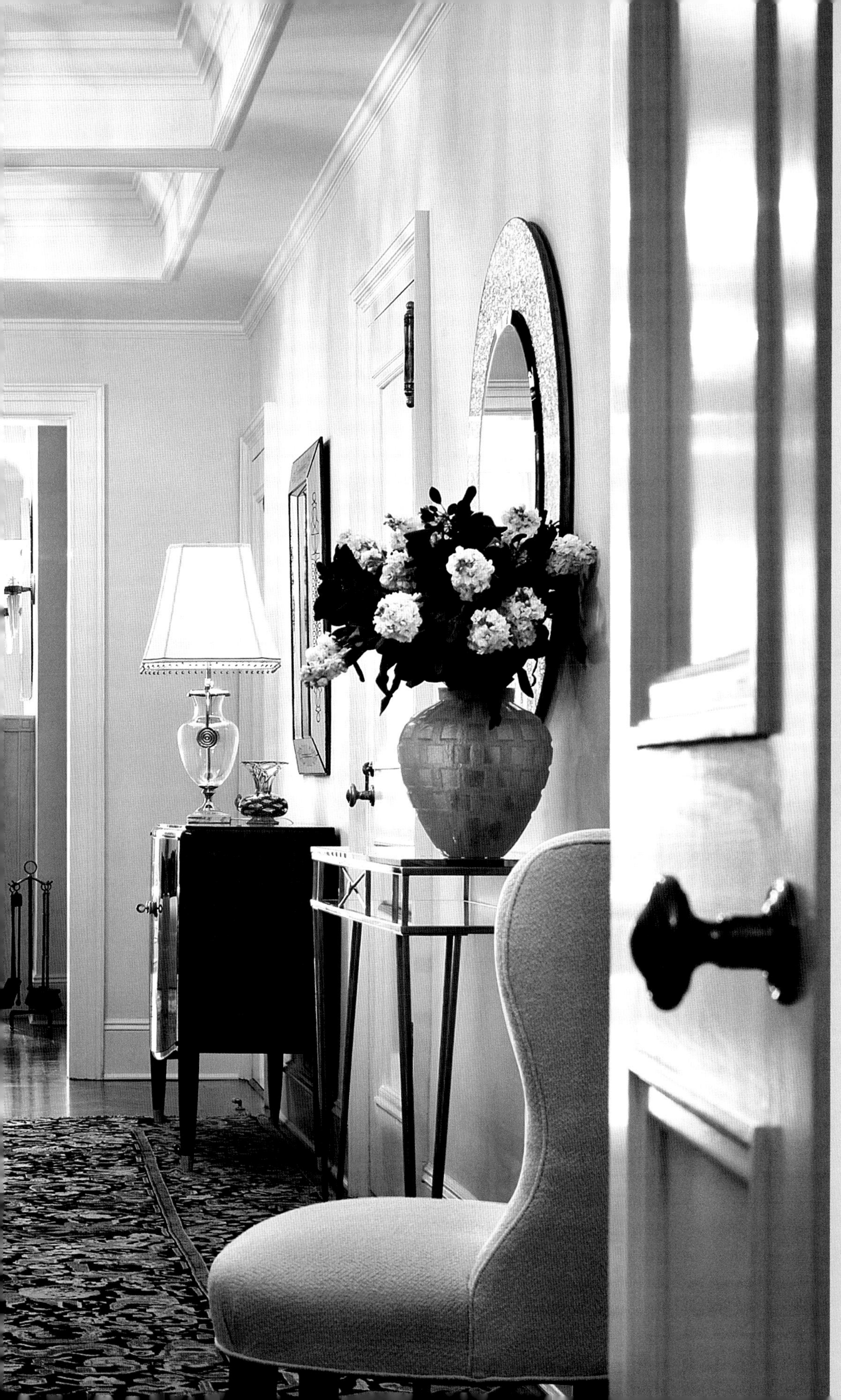

9 | TWO INTO ONE

I t is a truth universally acknowledged, that anyone living in a New York apartment must be in need of more space. So when my clients had the opportunity to acquire the apartment next door to theirs, they jumped at it. Jim Joseph was the architect who took on the job of combining the two apartments and did so in such a clever way that the results included more generous rooms and a separate wing for their three children.

The reconfigured entrance hall is now much larger, in scale with the rest of the apartment. An unusual coffered ceiling draws your eye up to appreciate the full height of the room. It's also one way to ensure that a long hall won't be boring. My daughter, Brooke, found the hanging lights, which are shaped like bell jars and made of delicate etched glass. They remind me of lace and cast interesting shadows. The rug is a real beauty. Its deep, rich colors ground the space. Two paintings by the same artist hang over two matching benches and establish a pleasing symmetry. But then we broke it on the other wall with mismatched mirrors over a table and a chest. Matched pairs on both walls would have been too tedious.

In the living room, the style is set by a collection of honey-colored French 1930s furniture. It's a cool, clean look. The square-back armchair and the sycamore cabinet have beautiful lines, and we designed the rest of the room in keeping with that period. The fireplace, from Jamb in London, is basically a creamy white rectangle with a slim top

PREVIOUS SPREAD

How nice to have enough room for seating in an entrance hall! The children can set down their backpacks and take off their boots while they perch for a moment on the matching benches that flank the door to their bedroom wing.

OPPOSITE

An accent color may come from a painting. Here, this picture is so prominent it became necessary to acknowledge its presence with pillows.

OVERLEAF

What's different about this living room? No picture over the mantel. No mirror. No bric-a-brac. Just two antique sconces. And that's enough. Empty space has its own beauty.

A ten-light chandelier diffuses the light over the dining table. Down the center, we grouped a collection of glassware, everything from candlesticks to vases. And then we added four roses. Isn't that more interesting than the typical bouquet? Two china cupboards made by Tommy Parzinger in the 1940s flank a modern burled-wood sideboard and give some weight to the wall opposite the fireplace.

instead of an overhanging mantel. It looks as if it could have been made by Jean-Michel Frank. The fire screen is fashioned after a Jean Royère original. The sofas and chairs we designed also have a 1930s feel, with softly rounded arms just elongated enough to make them interesting. It's lovely to have a room big enough to accommodate two large sofas and two oversize chairs in one seating group. Everybody should be very comfortable. The Venetian glass light fixture, also oversize and dusted with gold, was made by the fabled Archimede Seguso. It hangs in the center of the room and picks up the honey tones of the 1930s furniture. We also found a stripe with that same color for the curtains, which brings a lot of warmth to the room.

A slightly different stripe in the same tones was used for the curtains in the dining room. There are three adjacent windows that almost cover the whole wall, which makes curtains a little tricky. In order to have enough fabric to actually draw across each window, you have to stack it in between as well as at the sides. It's more complicated to do, but it creates a more period look than the alternative, which would be to treat the three as one big picture window. The other challenge in this room was the dining table. The clients wanted a table that could extend to seat twenty-four for Thanksgiving dinner. It's difficult to find such a large table made of a light-colored wood, so the furniture in this room is darker. The table we settled on is French, and the dining chairs are English. It's not easy to find a complete set of ten. We were lucky. The seats are covered in a persimmon-colored fabric. There's a reason for that. If you're using dark wood chairs around a dining table that's also dark, the upholstery on the chairs should be a little snappier, to brighten the mood.

The carpet picks up all the colors in the room and brings them all together. I often find myself buying the carpet first and then planning the colors of everything else around it. I first found that persimmon color in the rug and decided to use it for the chairs. The carpet in a room is a big investment, and it's crucial to the design. It's usually the largest field of color in the room, other than the walls. It has to have the right tones. When I find one I like, I'm tempted to buy it, even if I'm not quite sure what I'm going to do with it.

A family with three children needs a large family kitchen. The client is a good cook, and she knew exactly what kind of counters and cabinets and appliances she wanted. But this is not the typical white English scullery kitchen, so popular these days. Look at that lovely blue-flowered wallpaper. That was also chosen by Brooke, and it's very French. It gives the kitchen a whole new kind of coziness.

The accent color in the master bedroom is that same pale blue, seen in the bed linens and the Murano glass lamps on the dresser. The bench at the foot of the bed is exceptionally long and once graced an English hall. I chose that length in order to make the bench look as if it belonged with the width of the king-size bed. The bench's long, low lines also help break up the volume of the bed. At one end of the room, by the window, is a writing table that looks very French. The curtains are made of a tone-on-tone plaid. The walls are upholstered in damask in a slightly lighter shade.

These clients were able to carve a very large eat-in kitchen out of the combined apartments. Instead of a utilitarian breakfast table, they wanted a proper table and chairs. They take food and family meals very seriously. Did you notice the sofa? The kids can curl up and read. It's more conducive to conversation. I'm a proponent of good furniture, even in a kitchen.

OVERLEAF

In an otherwise vanilla room, I'll often introduce one shot of color. The important thing is to confine it to one color, like this pretty pale blue. That way, the room remains restful, which I think is essential in a bedroom. The furniture, the upholstered walls, and the carpet present an interesting mix of pattern, yet it's all relatively subtle, composed of similar tones on tones.

Even the wall-to-wall carpet has a subtle pattern. So you're enveloped in softness and cool, creamy colors, which makes for a very restful sleep (especially with the children all tucked into their own rooms, in another wing). It's a gift for a parent to have some privacy and solitude.

ABOVE LEFT

Powder rooms require the element of surprise. This one reminds you of the inside of a hatbox, with a large-scale rose-pattern paper by Ted Tyler, Italian sconces, and an outrageous piece of onyx.

ABOVE RIGHT

Most apartment powder rooms are interior spaces. A smart mosaic white-and-gray tile and white walls keep this one bright. Period nickel sconces and a Venetian mirror add glitter. The antique English washstand holds the sink. The mirror opens to a storage cabinet lined in mahogany matching the vanity.

RIGHT

Luxury for most people is a generously sized master bath. Here the bath and shower (not shown), vanity sink, dressing table, storage, and tile the color of water in the Caribbean wraps you in luxury.

First impressions count. I always make sure there's something interesting to look at as soon as you open the front door. The bookcase in the entryway of this apartment is made of the most beautiful wood, with a grain that radiates like a sunburst. See how the columns at the corners are tied with little brass strips? I believe this is a French piece, obviously one of a kind. The mirror is also French and dates from the 1940s. I like that pattern of interlocking bands on the frame. The whole composition invites you to come over to take a closer look. And the reflection in the mirror promises more to come.

Turn toward the living room, and the light from three large windows immediately draws you in. The windows are not all the same size because this room was made from two rooms put together. But the sheer white curtains mask this discrepancy and seem to embody the light. In any event, the room is really about that pure, pale wall of interlocking sycamore panels. It's a very clever way of changing the subject and was designed by the architect Stephen Wang. The panels, on concealed hinges, open to reveal all sorts of storage cabinets and music equipment and even a flat-screen TV.

The architecture is all about line and simplicity. So is the furniture. I made a point of choosing pieces with interesting profiles. That French 1930s chair is very seductive, with a swooping curve to the wood-framed

PREVIOUS SPREAD
The living room is composed of creams—on the walls, in the upholstery, in the carpet—but I've used black as the defining line. It outlines a shape without taking over. It's a neutral in its own way. White looks richer when you have the contrast of black; the black doesn't diminish the white but intensifies it.

OPPOSITE
You always need a focal point in an entrance hall. I like to create a little vignette, but that doesn't mean you need a lot of bits and bobs. All I wanted on top of this bookcase was one perfect vase that would look beautiful whether empty or filled with flowers. Notice that I didn't line up all the books in neat little rows. They attract more curiosity this way.

back and arms. It has a modern counterpart in that pair of contemporary wood-framed bergères. I upholstered them in chenille. Everybody loves chenille because it's so soft, and it's nice to have a soft fabric on a tight-backed chair. The sofa fabric has a little diamond pattern. When I'm doing the upholstery all in one color, I make sure to change the texture. The color of the upholstery blends into the color of the walls, which is one reason why the apartment feels so serene. But you can't simply fill a room with upholstered furniture. It would look like a blanket. That's why the wood-framed pieces are there. You need that contrast.

If you study the room, you'll notice that all the furniture is roughly the same height. This creates a very strong horizontal—a long, low

OPPOSITE

A two-tiered coffee table makes so much sense, especially for entertaining. The books can migrate to the lower level, making room on the top for hors d'oeuvres and a glass of wine. Actually, I tend to like anything with a shelf. Then I can keep a clean surface on top.

ABOVE

How wonderful—storage that's actually beautiful! For a moment you think this is just a paneled wall. The hardware is almost invisible. Hidden behind the sycamore panels are all sorts of things, including the audio-visual equipment. It's great to get all that paraphernalia out of the way.

horizon line. This is the other secret to making a room feel serene. The coffee table is like a calm pool in the middle. It's a big square with two tiers of glass, so instead of putting all your coffee table books on the top you can set them on the bottom and leave the top clear for coffee—or martinis.

The desk is right in the living room and placed so the person working at it can enjoy the view. Why tuck your desk away in a dark corner? Put it in a room where you want to be, and you'll use it more often. I had the desk copied from an art deco original. This way, we could have it outfitted for a computer and hide all the wires in the legs. It's made of mahogany with a very distinctive grain. Some people might wonder why I didn't make it out of the same sycamore as the wall panels just adjacent to it. The answer is simple: Because furniture is furniture and architecture is architecture. You don't want to conflate the

BELOW

The windows in the living room don't actually match, since it originally was two separate rooms. So the sheer white curtains are more about framing each half of the wall than treating each window individually. I like to orient a desk toward the view, rather than a blank wall.

OPPOSITE

The storage wall was very well thought out, with openings geared to whatever was going to be kept inside them. The TV is behind the two tall panels just to the left of center.

two. Besides, isn't it more interesting to see the dark wood against the light wall? In other words, don't hide your Cadillac. If you have an interesting piece, you might as well flaunt it and put it against a contrasting color that will bring out its shape and its lines.

A room will dictate how you should furnish it. You don't want to put a sofa in front of the window so you look into the room instead of out at the view. I always make sure a living room will seat eight or ten people. There should be a few different styles of chairs to choose from, some with tight backs and others with loose cushions, so a guest can pick the type of seating he or she prefers. You need a coffee table and some side tables so there's always a place to set down a book or a drink close by. And make sure you're designing the room to fit the way you want to use it.

The dining room here is the perfect example. The clients did not want a formal dining room, so we turned it into a much more intimate space with a small table and four leather club chairs. We built shelves for their books and storage cupboards that run the length of the wall. So it's more like a sitting room or a library. And yet, if needed, it can still be used for a dinner party. The table expands and the cupboards are just the right height to double as a sideboard. Multiuse, multifunction, multitasking—those are the key words today.

Look at the bedside table in the master bedroom. On it is a small TV so the husband can watch his program while his wife watches hers on the big screen. Or he can watch while she

OPPOSITE

The frosted-glass doors separating the living room from the library and dining room fold back, so you can make the space feel like one large room for a party. When the doors are partially closed, the library becomes a lovely spot for an intimate dinner. You could sit for hours in those comfortable chairs.

ABOVE

I call this an occasional kitchen. You don't really cook here; you just unwrap. In certain New York apartments that's all that's required, especially when you can walk out the door and down the block to your favorite restaurant. Wooden cabinets conceal almost everything. The backsplash is made of opaque glass.

OVERLEAF

In the master bedroom, the upholstered headboard blends right into the fabric-covered wall. In a small apartment, a hall is often the perfect place to tuck in some extra storage for books.

sleeps. Everybody has his own idea of what the perfect bedroom should be. Some people love to see light in the morning. Others want blackout curtains on all the windows. Some people like a bed with a footboard. Others like to be able to perch on the end of the bed. Everybody wants at least one comfy upholstered chair where you can sit for a moment and take off your shoes. Because I love to read in bed, I like an upholstered headboard, and so do these clients. The one I made for them is channeled, so it feels vaguely art deco, in keeping with the style of the rest of the furniture in the apartment.

The master bath is a limestone-lined retreat. The tub is long enough so that a person can lie back and relax. The shower is encased in frosted glass. But look what found its way into this calm, quiet atmosphere—the treadmill. And another TV set. What did I say? It's all about multitasking. These days, when apartment space is so scarce and expensive, it makes sense to use rooms in multiple ways.

OPPOSITE

The unique feature in this bathroom, besides the treadmill, is the recessed waterfall over the tub. A simple pump forces water up over a sheet of glass, where it then falls and cycles back. That splashing water suddenly puts you in the midst of nature. You're missing only the chirping birds.

ABOVE

In this powder room the walls are upholstered in silk above a painted wainscot and a square sink recessed in a bamboo floating counter.

OCEANFRONT PURITY

What is the mantra of every single real estate broker you've ever met? Location, location, location. Get that right, and nothing else really matters because almost anything else can be changed—with the help of a good designer. This apartment definitely presented a challenge when I first walked in the door. It was a sea of mirrored walls and marble flooring, but it was on the ocean in Palm Beach, Florida. Right at the water's edge. Need I say more?

The first changes I wanted to make were obvious to me. We took down all the mirrors and covered the walls in a smooth coat of creamy white paint. We removed all the marble and poured a simple concrete floor. Concrete is a good example of an inexpensive material that can look great, just by changing the context. Art dealers quickly figured this out, and concrete floors have become a given in chic galleries. This client is an artist and an art collector who appreciates the beauty of simple materials. And concrete makes so much sense by the beach. Sand and moisture won't harm it. Even on the hottest day, it stays cool underfoot.

My next intervention required a little more contemplation and involved an immovable object—a large column—smack in the middle of

PREVIOUS SPREAD
Sliding glass doors at one end of the dining room open to a patio at the water's edge. The clients can eat outside when the weather's fine. An overhang shelters them from the sun. And the outdoor furniture lasts longer since it's not completely exposed to the elements.

OPPOSITE
A pair of unique Danish modern chairs sits in front of a lacquered wood piece by Edward Wormley. This sideboard houses good storage behind doors sporting the designer signature finger pulls. A collection of geometric forms sits below a modern painting.

OVERLEAF
Instead of trying to ignore an awkward column in the entryway, I covered it in stainless steel and transformed it into a focal point. Then I added a sleek stainless-steel shelf, which connects back to the wall and offers a place for a welcoming vase of flowers. The minimalist sofa just beyond is by Florence Knoll.

the entrance hall. I couldn't exactly hide it, so I decided to play it up instead. Why not turn it into an art piece? I sheathed it in stainless steel and then ran a slim stainless steel shelf from it to the wall. It looks great and provides a handy place to put down your keys. I love this little ledge. For me, it sums up the whole apartment, which is about simplicity, purity, and the beauty of negative space.

There are only a few well-chosen pieces in each room. Mid-century modern furniture was the logical place to start because I knew the art the client owned was from that same period. I chose a sleek, linear sofa designed by Florence Knoll for the entryway. The living room has a wall of floor-to-ceiling windows facing the ocean, and I wanted pieces that held their own but did not compete with the view. I designed a pair of comfortable sofas and upholstered them in a gray-beige fabric that seems

to pick up its tones from the concrete. Then I added two Danish modern cane-back chairs and two armchairs that date to the 1950s. The coffee table is a massive rectangle made of cork—very sculptural. All the pieces have strong lines—long and low, like the horizon line of the ocean in the distance. The upholstery is in cool, neutral tones. Everything is very understated. The thing I want people to remember

When I see a place like this, right by the ocean, I really want to be outside. The glass wall in the living room makes you feel as if you already are. When the view is this good, I don't see any reason why the furniture should compete, so I kept the arrangement very simple and straightforward.

OVERLEAF

You know how much I like negative space. I grouped the furniture in these rooms to leave plenty of it. The concrete floors are kept purposefully bare in the circulation areas, while a rug softens the seating area.

about this room is that view of sea and sky. I didn't want to fill these rooms with furniture. I wanted them to be filled with light and air.

The dining room is a composition of shapes—the square-back chairs, the octagonal table, the rectangular sideboard—and then the paintings add color. In the master bedroom, we kept it equally simple, with a long, low bed and a plain rectangular upholstered headboard. Then I put a wide wooden frame on it, just to say hello to all the other wood. The bedside tables are also my design, and for this house, I topped them with a slab of stone, which feels clean and adds a contemporary touch.

It was interesting to take another look at midcentury modern while I was doing this apartment. It's the kind of furniture many people grew up with, and frankly, a lot of it is not all that memorable. But the most talented designers were making beautiful pieces—strong, sharp-edged, very spare and modern. If you put them in a compatible space, like this cool, clean apartment by the water, they finally get to sing their song.

The sculpture, by the owner, gives a counterpoint to the collection of 1950s artists.

OVERLEAF
The master bedroom is sparely furnished, imparting an appealing quietness. The slim desk near the window has a particularly interesting profile, which is why I made sure you first see it from the side. A huge pocket door slides back to make the room feel even more spacious.

The apartment's master bedroom holds a
rosewood and lacquer double dresser. The
mirror extends the room and can be used
on the way out for a last-minute look-see.

Nothing warms up an apartment quite like antiques. The patina of old burnished wood that has been waxed and polished and cherished for centuries just can't be beat. This apartment belongs to a woman who has a great eye for antiques. She's a collector, and she likes to live with her collections in plain view. She doesn't believe in keeping her treasures roped off or hidden away.

Take that Chippendale chair in her library. It's the real thing, with intricately carved ball-and-claw feet. It's pulled up to a small pedestal table right in the middle of the room, ready for anyone to sit in it. Good furniture was made to be used. It has lasted for many years and will survive for many more. There's no reason to be afraid of it. My client will sit down and unfold the writing table that's built into that fine American secretary that dates from 1850. She keeps various papers stored in the nooks and crannies behind those doors. The secretary is a nineteenth-century version of the twenty-first-century home office. Compact, convenient, and beautiful at the same time.

That could also describe a pair of Paul McCobb chests in the living room. They're from a completely different period, a hundred years later,

PREVIOUS SPREAD
The recess here creates an interesting depth in the apartment foyer, and the mirror and recessed light catches your eye.

OPPOSITE
The living room and the library are separated by pocket doors. They may be old-fashioned, but they really work, taking up relatively little space and affording a lot of privacy.

OVERLEAF
This is the kind of apartment where you can be yourself. It's so comfortable and easy. You don't have to confine yourself to furniture from the same period or style. You can have printed fabrics next to a check. In fact, you can have anything you want. This apartment represents a lovely sort of freedom.

but they have an equal amount of integrity and their own strong lines. The furniture in this room reminds me of a group of old friends. Each piece has its own character and is upholstered in its own particular pattern. The two club chairs covered in the Bennison floral print are obviously twins. Other pieces sport a gingham check, a stripe, and a ribbed chenille, which should convince anyone that, yes, I can actually do prints and patterns when I want to. The rug is North Indian and brings in more browns, creams, blues, and grays. There are no curtains on the windows, just wooden shutters. They feel clean and crisp, and suggest a certain early American simplicity.

On one wall, I hung a great big English mirror over a drop-leaf table. In geometric terms, it forms a rectangle over a half-circle. I love those kinds of relationships. In school, I wasn't good at algebra, but I was a whiz at geometry. I'm still playing around with shapes. I guess I do it unconsciously. I always think in terms of balance and proportion, and I won't leave a room until I feel the balance is right. I will stand there and study the arrangement of furniture and perhaps move a lamp to one side, to try and fix it. It's something that's hard to explain rationally. I just do it by eye.

Each room is a composition, and once you have resolved the relationships among all the objects, the room feels complete.

ABOVE

In apartments, strive to use every inch. In the library-study, a vertical tower more useful for a collection of mochaware than books is an eye teaser!

OPPOSITE

Doors need character that measures up to any room of quality. Even this door to the small kitchen uses a raised panel.

OVERLEAF

A small sofa serves as a banquette for an informal meeting and late lunch, or enjoying a book on a quiet afternoon. Louvered shutters adjust the quality of the light.

I'm not fond of master bedrooms that consist of just four walls and a bed. That can feel very unbalanced and much too spare. Here, we added built-in storage cabinets. But instead of filling up the whole wall, we separated them into two sections, with a built-in dressing table in between. The recess above and below the table, where we tucked in a bench, adds more depth to the room and makes it feel less like a box. This room, too, has layers upon layers of pattern. It starts with the walls, which are covered in strié silk, and moves on to the headboard, which is embroidered with flowers. A tone-on-tone white crewel covers a chair. Even the rug is embossed. It just goes to show that pattern doesn't have to mean chintz. I had one chintz in my life, made by Rose Cumming, but when I tried to order more of it I discovered that it had been discontinued. I have never found another that I like as much.

But that doesn't mean I've given up on pattern. As this room proves, you can have patterns that are built out of texture and subtlety, rather than strong, contrasting colors. I find that more restful. Forget the bright chintz. I'm sticking with that creamy crewel.

LEFT

The drop-leaf table can be pulled out and opened for a large dinner party, but I like it even better closed. Paired with a mahogany mirror, it forms a strong geometric composition.

OVERLEAF

Everything in this comfortable master bedroom is covered in either silk, cotton, linen, or wool. Natural fabrics are the simplest of luxuries, and to complement them, all you need is one memorable moment in a room. Here, for me, it's the weathervane. I love the silhouette it forms in front of the shutters. That little bit of darkness against the light is like a period. The end.

ouldn't we all like to live in a ballroom? These clients actually do. The building in Palm Beach, Florida, was originally a hotel, and their ground-floor apartment was formerly the ballroom. That's why it's on such a grand scale, with immensely tall ceilings and floor-to-ceiling French doors that frame splendid views of the Intracoastal Waterway. To make such a large space livable required a special hand. We needed to turn size into serenity.

The entrance hall came with a circular cove in the ceiling, lit with unseen lights to create a celestial glow. That's a clever way to bring light into an interior room. We kept it and supplemented it with a pair of Venetian glass chandeliers. I found a beautiful Japanese screen for the wall, which brings a certain warmth and stillness to the room. The gold leaf shimmers in the light. The screen hangs above a wrought iron console that looks as if it could have been made in the 1920s or the 1930s, but is actually a contemporary piece. It's topped with stone. The floors throughout the apartment are also stone—so cooling in the Florida heat.

Like many entrance halls, this one is designed to borrow light from the adjacent rooms. A wide doorway leads to the living room,

PREVIOUS SPREAD
I think a room this large should use something of a similar scale, and with twelve panels, the coromandel screen fits the bill and wraps around the alcove. Its delicious color—somewhere between bitter chocolate and aubergine—creates an intriguing play of dark and light.

OPPOSITE
When you have a large space like this entrance hall, you really need large-scale furnishings. The console table is big. The Japanese screen is big. They also bring in some patina, which counteracts the coolness of the stone floor.

OVERLEAF
The two main seating areas are connected by matching coffee tables made in the style of Jean Royère, with a delicate diamond-patterned metal grid. All the furniture is upholstered in similar pale shades, but if you look closely you'll notice a subtle mix of texture and pattern. The curtains are simple so they don't interfere with the view.

which is flooded with sunlight from the French doors that practically wrap the space. Pale vanilla-colored curtains in a lovely thick woven cotton hang from the ceiling, which must be twelve feet high, and soften the bright light. The furniture is placed to enjoy the view. The room is so huge that it could easily accommodate two seating areas, each the size of a normal living room. The clients do a lot of entertaining, and they really use this space. The sofas and chairs are upholstered in pale vanilla, like the walls, which creates a restful atmosphere. The coffee table, made in the style of Jean Royère, is a simple diamond-patterned metal grid topped with glass. It's barely there. In a warm climate, I think you want things to feel light and airy.

Yet you still need something to ground the space and keep everything from floating off into the stratosphere. An antique coromandel screen performs that function here. It's made of twelve intricately patterned panels, but the base color is a deep, rich brown. It looks as if it was once black and has faded over the centuries. It's got a bit of red in it, and aubergine, which gives it more depth. It's a great operatic moment in the apartment. On one side, you look out and see the water. On the other, you see this magnificent screen. It adds history, quality, and connoisseurship. There's something about its darkness that is intriguing in this white, white room. Because the sun is so bright you get the purity and dazzle of all the white. Somehow the dark screen makes the white look even whiter, even as it calms the interior. And then I added a big leather ottoman so everyone can put his or her feet up. It's a little unexpected, a little different. Not white, for one thing, and that odd-man-out quality is what makes it work for me. An ottoman upholstered in white, like the rest of the furniture, would have been too predictable.

The dining room is very interesting. It's shaped like an oval, which immediately draws your attention and makes you feel as though

you've entered a very special room. It is furnished with two dining tables rather than one because it's more flexible that way. Both tables extend, so you can seat a dinner party of eight or twenty-four comfortably. I covered the walls in a striped silk, which was tricky to do on a curved surface but well worth the extra effort. Fabric-covered walls really warm up a room and make a large space feel cozy.

Since the master bedroom is also large, we decided to cover those walls with fabric, too, and chose an ivory-and–café au lait silk plaid. It adds a little texture and helps pull the space together as it wraps the room. I wanted to soften the stone floor with a rug and chose one with a large floral pattern to suit the scale of the room. Before we bought it, I arranged to have it shipped to Palm Beach so we could lay it out in the bedroom and see how the colors—ivory, pale green, and aubergine—looked in the bright Florida sun. I highly recommend doing this because the way a rug looks in the showroom and your house can be very different.

The bed is upholstered, which also helps soften the room. The clients really didn't need much else because storage was taken care of in the adjacent dressing rooms and their desks were in their studies. But I did convince the wife that there was one piece of furniture that could make the room—a dramatically overscale chaise. It holds

OPPOSITE

There's a carved wood detail on the doors leading to the master bedroom, and another lovely detail on the curtains—a whimsical fringe trim.

ABOVE

The master bedroom is all about large scale and luxury. Strong, rich silk fabrics grab your attention before you realize the height of the ceiling.

OVERLEAF

The bed is substantial, and even the pattern on the rug is overscale to suit the scale of the room. Etched glass doors lead to his-and-hers dressing rooms.

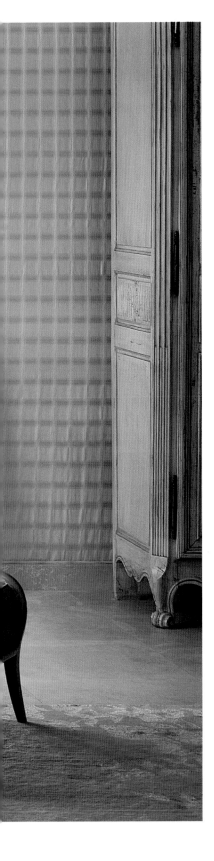

its own in a windowed corner opposite the bed and balances out the room.

Those floor-to-ceiling windows mean that everywhere you turn there is another magnificent view. But the boundary between indoors and out really blurs on the patio, which is roofed and open to the breeze, with striped canvas curtain panels in lieu of walls. It's a glorious outdoor room, furnished with big, comfortable wicker chairs and sofas. You can sit and contemplate the water or the sky, with the city across the way. It almost feels as if the waves come right up to the door. What a wonderful way to live. It's hard to believe that this is actually someone's apartment.

This chaise frame is made of an exotic holly wood (a pale blondish wood) and has a channeled tufted back and luxuriously upholstered seat. We paired it with an equally beautiful large-scale glass floor lamp. In a way, its generous size and style might be right at home in a Fred Astaire and Ginger Rogers 1930s film.

The guiding concept, whether you're merely redecorating or doing a gut renovation, should be to bring out your own personality. Choose furnishings that have meaning for you. The objects someone collects are a glimpse into his or her soul. Those very individual items are what make a place memorable.

Remember, first impressions please or distract, and that happens right inside the apartment's front door. The main event is how you see the beginning and then how you carry those themes through each and every room. Plan for continuity and originality. Layer each room with color and texture combinations that are subtle yet powerful. The most successful interiors, in my opinion, combine traditional and modern pieces into a mix that embodies your own personal style. Incorporate old friends into your furniture arrangements and a few newly chosen ones as well. Acknowledge history and even add a little humor. Make your apartment warm. Make it your home.

AFTERWORD

Like any good apartment, a book requires enormous effort and teamwork. I would like to thank my good friend, photographer Scott Frances, for capturing the brilliant images contained in this book. Once again, Christine Pittel used her stellar talent, creativity, and reflection in constructing a meticulous narrative. My gratitude to all the architectural collaborators mentioned throughout the text: Jim Joseph of Hottenroth & Joseph (Chapters 1 and 9), Ferguson-Shamamian Architects (Chapter 3), Boris Baranovich (Chapter 6), Mark Simon of Centerbrook Architects (Chapter 7), Peter Cook (Chapter 8), Stephen J. Wang (Chapter 10), and Lori Shields (Chapter 12). Their cumulative knowledge and innovative abilities continue to educate my own process. Many thanks to another friend, James Mortimer, for supplying the photography in the "European-Style" chapter. The book simply could not have been possible without the patience, pristine organization, and research skills of Mary Dobbin, Renee Infantino, and Karen Laurence. I also extend my gratitude to the staff at Gomez Associates for all their enthusiasm and talents. Thanks to Pam Bernstein, who has been a longtime friend, colleague, and supporter. To everyone at HarperCollins, including Cassie Jones and Marta Schooler; their outstanding editing skills, direction, and counsel made the process effortless and pleasurable. My deep appreciation to Joel Avirom for his astounding, sophisticated, and inventive design; each page is more beautiful than the next. Exceptional thanks to Paige Rense for her longtime contribution to the world of design, and her encouragement and support as a friend.

ACKNOWLEDGMENTS